The Na[r] Abuse F Guide

CW00499518

The 6 Step System to Survive and Thrive After Gaslighting, Codependency, and Unhealthy Emotional Relationships

Denise King

Table of Contents

Introduction

Am I crazy? NO. Well, I have mood swings… and sometimes, I forget to put my cup in the sink when I'm done or miss the laundry basket. Of course, there were those few times I said the wrong thing in front of our friends… I guess I am a bit of a bad person, and I make their lives difficult. I mean, look at how much they do for me. Not only do they accept all my flaws, but they look after me, care for me, and help me whenever they can. I guess I should be happy… so why am I not?

Let's be honest, it is almost impossible to find someone that hasn't had a conversation with themselves like this. The problem? Not everyone realizes what they actually went through, and even fewer of them will talk about it publicly.

As a survivor of narcissistic abuse, it still feels like narcissists control the world. Often, when I would talk to friends, family members, and sometimes random strangers, they would make it clear they had been through the same thing. But, when I would try to approach them for a conversation—because honestly, if you cannot accept it and talk about it, you cannot move on from it— Instead of talking to me about it, these people would close down and excuse themselves from the conversation. Some people feel so ashamed about being victims of narcissistic abuse that they either go into denial or they accept and bury it. Don't get me wrong, if this is what they need to do to cope, that is completely fine. Hopefully in the future they will open up about it when they are ready. However, some people like me need to talk about it and bring it into the open, and we need others to go through it with so we know that we are not alone.

This book will be about helping those that have suffered from abuse find a way to let go, heal, and move forward. I want to help people realize that it is okay that you went through this; it is not your fault. You will move on, you will heal, and you will trust someone again. You will find someone that actually, really and truly loves you, and yes, you will find someone that you will feel the same way about.

You have gone through a horrible experience, but I can promise you that it will be okay. As I said, I am a survivor of narcissistic abuse; I experienced it first hand, and then I decided to research it and learn whatever I could. As I researched, it occurred to me that I am not the only one who has gone through this. Like many others, including you considering you've decided to read this book, I had to gain information; I had to figure out how to move on, and then I had to share what I learned to possibly help others. This is part of my healing, this is part of rebuilding myself and correcting the indiscretions I found were committed against me.

I am not alone. You are not alone. Together we can make it! Together we can create a family, find ourselves again, and repair the damage that was caused to us. We can find happiness again, and the best thing about it is that we don't have to overexert and completely deplete our energies to do so.

We'll go on a journey together and rediscover ourselves. We'll break away from their abuse and find our freedom. We'll learn how they think and we'll learn how to actually leave them. We'll do it together, and make sure that we are okay throughout the entire process.

I am not writing this book to tell you what to do, but rather as a friend, going through it with you, knowing how you are feeling, and working with you. Let's get started and take back our lives.

Chapter 1:

Into the World of

Narcissism

It is so hard to heal and move on from something if we don't understand why it happened or even how. The same applies to narcissistic abuse. I found that as soon as I understood the narcissist better—where they came from and what their own history was, especially the history they never told me about—that it all suddenly clicked into place for me; it was the epiphany moment that had me go "aha!" Before we get too far, I felt it was important to share what I learned about narcissism. This will allow us to begin to understand the origins of our pain.

The Narcissism Overview

Narcissism feels so common, it feels like I can throw a rock into a crowd and hit ten people that have been affected by narcissists, and unsurprisingly most of them will be women as 75% of people diagnosed with Narcissistic Personality Disorder (NPD) are men.

Imagine my surprise when I found out that only 1 in 200 people in the United States actually has NPD.

It is quite common for everyone to have at least a few narcissistic traits. In fact, it is even healthy for most teenagers to display these qualities as part of their development. Social media has also had a huge impact on NPD and its reach. It allows narcissists to reach more people in different social environments and also encourages narcissism.

The Two Main Types of Narcissism

Adaptive Narcissism

We have all heard about narcissism and what a negative thing it is. Meeting a narcissist is like riding a rollercoaster. The moment you get in that car, you know you are going up; as the car goes higher and your anticipation grows you get more and more excited. You already love the idea of this is. But then when you reach peak you see this drop, and you know you can't stop it. Fear sets in and the drop happens even faster than the build-up. Before you know it you are screaming at the top of your lungs, a few swear words slip out, and you know you messed up because everyone around you will silently judge you for the rest of the ride, but you can't help it. As the rollercoaster goes on, it doesn't really slow down, but the heights get small, the twists and turns get scarier, and before you know it, your ride is over. Now you have to get off so someone else can take your spot. You walk away from it, and as scared as you were, as sick as it made you, you miss it. The few fleeting moments you spent on that rollercoaster felt like a lifetime, and maybe you are too scared to get on again, but a part of you will always long for that excitement again. You may even look at the next group of people start taking that first high peak and feel a bit of jealousy. This is how we feel after an encounter with a narcissist. The relationship mimics a rollercoaster ride quite intently. So imagine my surprise when I first learned that there is good narcissism. I started to think about it, and the term "a healthy ego" popped into my head. This is exactly what adaptive narcissism is. This is someone who has found that sweet spot between having enough self-esteem without having an inflated ego, who has found a healthy way to think about themselves. They do not have an issue with low self-esteem or self-importance. Being an adaptive narcissist is the only good type of narcissist there is.

Maladaptive Narcissism

This is the negative kind of narcissism that we have gotten used to. These are the entitled and abusive ones. This is the unhealthy type of narcissism which will usually be diagnosed as Narcissistic Personality Disorder. It's because of this that the five types of narcissism experts usually refer to, all fall under this umbrella.

Five Sub-Types of Narcissism

Think of Narcissism being like a berry. Blueberries and Mistletoe are both berries, but there is a major contrast in taste and effect from them. They grow in different environments and look different, but they are still berries. The five types of narcissism are the same.

Overt Narcissism

When I say narcissist, this is normally the type of narcissist you will think of. This is also called grandiose narcissism. Those who fall under this type usually display extreme extrovert personality traits. These will be outgoing, arrogant, entitled people that need to be praised and admired constantly and will be extremely competitive while lacking empathy. A 2018 study also found that overt narcissism can also cause someone to overestimate their own emotional intelligence.

Covert Narcissism

A covert narcissist—also known as vulnerable or closet narcissism—will normally be in direct contrast to an overt narcissist. These are the people that get all the attention on them by playing the victim or telling you how they are not good enough. They tend to get extremely defensive. I realize this sounds like they may not be narcissistic at all, but the key is that they only focus on themselves. Two people can be in the exact same situation. For example, being stranded in a foreign country with no means of identification or way to contact anyone for help. They may both be scared, unsure, and extremely stressed out, but the covert narcissist will act like they are the only victim, they are the only one to go through this; they are the only scared one, and will completely disregard the emotions and needs of the other person. They have to be worse off, and you have to feel sorry for them. You also cannot criticize someone with covert narcissism in any way because they will immediately feel that it was harsher than you intended it to be.

In 2017, a study found that covert narcissism tends to link strongly to high neuroticism. Other research also suggests that covert and overt narcissism may not be mutually exclusive, but that they could form part of a cycle that the narcissist goes through.

Antagonistic Narcissism

Some research has indicated that antagonistic narcissism could be a subtype of overt narcissism, this will mean that those with overt narcissism will focus more on the competitive aspects of their personality. They will tend to be more arrogant and argumentative as well. Different studies from 2017 and 2019 have found that those with antagonistic narcissism may also be less likely to forgive someone, while also having lower levels of trust in others.

Communal Narcissism

When someone is a communal narcissist, they tend to see themselves as altruistic. They will believe that they are extremely empathic and generous, and have extreme reactions when they perceive something as unfair or feel morally outraged. This all sounds good, right? The issue comes in when there is a major difference between their beliefs and their behavior. Think of someone that will make a show of telling people to give to the poor, donate to animal rescues and support charities, but never actually practice this themselves. They may even contradict themselves when they think nobody is around.

Malignant Narcissism

Malignant narcissism is so severe that it can often cause problems for the narcissists themselves as well. They will likely be an aggressive and vindictive individual that is sadistic and enjoys the pain of others, and they may also be extremely paranoid. They usually share many personality traits with antisocial personality disorder, and this can lead them to having legal and substance abuse problems.

The Causes of Narcissism

Now that we understand the types of narcissists we can encounter, we need to look at what causes people to suffer from narcissism. There are many similarities in the history and lives of people that have NPD. These similarities range from their childhood to environments to genetics. The problem is that it is still extremely difficult to pinpoint the exact cause of NPD. Some believe it to be a product of nurture, directly caused by the environment around a child, and the actions of their guardians and authority figures around them in their formative years.

Since all three beliefs carry their own weight, I felt it important to look at all three theories. We'll start at looking into the environment theory as this is the most accepted theory at the moment.

The theory is that a variety of different aspects and influences can cause a child to grow up and experience NPD. The largest impact would be children that suffer from trauma—whether this trauma is more direct like a physically abusive authority figure, an accident, or something more indirect like an emotionally abusive authority figure, the result is often the same. Abuse is, however, not the only environmental factor believed to cause NPD, but a neglectful or emotionally absent parent or guardian, as well as a overbearing guardian that supplies an excessive amount of praise has also been linked as possible causes.

There is, however, a large enough amount of narcissists whom do not show signs of a traumatic history. These are the ones that have caused the theory on genetics and neurobiology to take rise. In 2014, a study was conducted on twins that found that narcissistic traits are at least somewhat inheritable. These are traits such as grandiosity, entitlement and neuroticism. These traits could, however, exist separately from NPD or could also be the most prominent traits in someone with NPD.

It is also important to note here that the belief is that the seeds of narcissism get planted at a young age. Even if the cause is a hereditary predisposition or a pre-existing genetic marker, these are activated in the formative years where a child needs to learn to bully or manipulate those around them in order to make sure that their own needs are met. They might be so used to this behavior that they integrate this in their adult relationships. They also may not realize that they are narcissists themselves.

The Traits of a Narcissist

Now that we know where narcissism comes from, and we know or at least suspect that we have already encountered at least one type of narcissist, we need to look at all the traits of narcissism to be sure we are prepared and can identify a narcissist if we encounter them or may already have encountered them. To start off, with I would like for us to have a look at the 12 signs of narcissism.

Inflated Sense of Self

The person will feel that they are superior to others, and that this superiority entitles them to better and special treatment. They will also tend to revert to fantasies of having unlimited success, beauty, power, and love.

Need for Adoration

A narcissist will always try to monopolize the conversation and steer it to ensure that they are the center of attention. When they do not achieve this goal, they will become enraged and feel mistreated and depleted. When a narcissist does this, they make you feel like you cannot get a word in edgewise, or that you are constantly being interrupted and talked over. Has a partner ever made you feel like your opinions or viewpoints don't matter to them? If you answered yes, then the chances are very good that you are dealing with a narcissist.

Exploiting Relationships

For a narcissist, a relationship is not based on emotional connections, but instead on the perceived benefits that the narcissist can enjoy from this relationship. The more unique skills and attributes you have, the more valuable you are to them and the more they will build this relationship with you.

Need for Control

Much like their need for adoration and to be the center of attention, the narcissist has a need to control every situation around them. They will often appear as a perfectionist that gets aggravated and upset when something does not go their way.

Lack of Empathy

It should come as no surprise that a lack of empathy has made the list, but it has, and we still need to look at it. A narcissist has little to no empathy for others. They almost completely lack the ability to care about the emotions and experiences of those close to them.

Identity Disturbance

The narcissist only remains stable as long as they believe themselves to be exceptional. If they are faced with a reality that challenges or straight out denies this view that a narcissist has, they will shy away from it in order to protect their own fragile self-image.

Intimacy Problems

The narcissist will tend to stay away from intimate relationships. Even when they do enter in close relationships, these will usually be void of intimacy. The only use outside of their direct benefits from a relationship is to help their own self image.

Boredom

In any situation in which the attention is not on the narcissist they will find boring and become restless and depressed. When they are not in the spotlight, it shines too bright for them. If they don't feel taken aback by this, they will feel indifferent and not see the reason for someone else being praised.

Difficulty Accepting Challenges

One of the first possible signs exhibited by narcissists is "failure to launch" syndrome. This occurs during the transition phase where a teen becomes a young adult, where they have to attend college or university, or start working full-time jobs and have to live on their own. A narcissist is more prone to resisting these changes, and will often regress in their maturity and require sustained support over a long period of time, usually from their parents. Later in life, this will also become apparent when they often feel overwhelmed by their jobs, school or relationships, especially when they have difficulty delivering realistic goals.

No Responsibility

When something goes wrong, it will never be the fault of the narcissist. They will blame others for something that may clearly be their fault, and usually very convincingly. The blame will usually be pushed to those closest to them.

No Boundaries

The narcissist always knows better; therefore, you should always be thinking like them and taking their advice. This is what they believe and why they will often insert themselves into the lives and situations of those around them, even if it is not their place to be there. If anyone should tell them not to or disagree in any way, the narcissist will be shocked and feel insulted by this.

Fear of Rejection

I'm a bit skeptical to use the word fear, as it is less of a fear and more of a refusal to be rejected. Their entire personality is built around being important and being the center of attention. That is why they will do whatever they can to not be rejected. This is also the reason why they do not develop any trust in the love of others.

Narcissist Checkbox

As we know by now, narcissists can be quite beguiling in the beginning and can manipulate us so subtly that we do not realize what is happening until we are hooked. So if we have a checklist that can help us spot a narcissist early on, we could use it to our advantage.

Below, you will find a list of nine traits that are used to determine whether a person has NPD. If they tick off five of the nine traits, they are considered to have NPD. As we are not mental health experts, we cannot clearly define whether or not a person actually has these personality traits, but if we do suspect them of at least five of these traits, it may be a good idea to distance ourselves from them.

The traits are:

- Having a grandiose sense of self-importance.

- An inflated sense of entitlement.

- Being preoccupied with fantasies of unlimited success, fame, or beauty.

- Believing that they are extremely special and unique to the point where normal people cannot understand them. Only those as special and unique as they are can understand them.

- Constantly requiring an excessive amount of admiration.

- Exploiting and taking advantage of others on a constant basis.

- Having very little or a complete lack of empathy towards others.

- Either being constantly envious of others, or believing that others are constantly envious of them.

- Being extremely arrogant.

Scientific Facts About Narcissistic Personality Disorder

Now although we already have a pretty good understanding of what a real narcissist is, we need to face some misconception and false information that is out there. Don't feel bad if you find that you have fallen victim to this misinformation, we all have. The only way we can get the real truth is by researching.

Narcissism Is on a Spectrum

As with most other personality disorders, narcissism exists on a spectrum. This spectrum can range from someone only displaying narcissistic tendencies to full-blown NPD. Narcissistic tendencies can become more obvious when the person is under stress, but it only becomes a disorder when these tendencies are experienced continuously.

Narcissists Are Not Necessarily Self-Indulgent

It is often believed that narcissists are all completely over-indulgent. This is not true; however, and the traits of a narcissist can very quickly become a problem for the narcissist themselves.

Characterized as Oversized Self-Esteem

Narcissists have a sense of oversized self-confidence that is used to cover up their own pain, guilt and embarrassment, this is why Narcissists have such a difficulty handling criticism.

It's Not Entirely Clear How Common NPD Is

It is estimated that 0 to 6.2% of the global population has NPD, according to the Diagnostic and Statistical Manual of Mental Disorders, 5th Edition, commonly referred to as the DSM-5 (or as I refer to it: this mouthful of words). This number appears to be extremely low. The reason for this could be the fact that research into NPD is extremely lacking and a lot more research is required to definitively establish just how common NPD is.

More Common in Men Than in Women

A variety of studies have found that even though men and women are equally as self absorbed, men tend to show more narcissistic traits. However, more studies are required.

Experts Are Not Sure Exactly What Causes NPD

The main idea at the moment is that NPD is akin to alcoholism, where a person may have a genetic predisposition to it, which will cause a larger chance to develop NPD, but that environmental factors may increase or decrease their chance of developing this disorder. But again, further research is required to establish this completely.

NPD Can Be Tough to Diagnose

NPD can only be diagnosed by a mental health expert during adulthood as adolescents could be extremely self-involved while growing up. There are no lab tests that can detect NPD so, the only way to determine that someone has NPD is by use of a questionnaire filled out through a series of interviews.

Therapy Can Help Someone With NPD

There are no medications to treat NPD, which contributes to why NPD is one of the hardest psychiatric conditions to treat. The best way to treat NPD is with therapy. The problem is that a narcissist will normally do whatever they can to avoid a situation in which they will be told that they are wrong, and this definitely includes therapy.

NPD Is Widely Misunderstood

Quite often, someone that is simply a spoiled person will be labeled a narcissist even though they usually do not possess more than one or two narcissistic traits. The term narcissist can be overly used by the general population until they actually encounter a real narcissist.

Chapter 2:

You and the Narcissist

Survivor of Narcissism

In this scenario, our survivor had met the narcissist when they were introduced by a mutual friend. The survivor's initial impression of the narcissist was that he was not her type at all. The narcissist did not appear to have the type of personality that she would normally get along with. However, within a few hours, he had changed her mind. He had even made her worry and care for him by sharing stories of his own troubled childhood. He told her that they have a lot in common. Their dreams, their fears, their insecurities, and their interests. It was like he was made just for her. Within a few days, the narcissist had used a technique called love bombing so effectively that she described him as her entire world already.

By a month later, he completely changed. He had already established power over her so he could do whatever he wanted to now. He started by staying away from her for days, where he would completely ignore her, and would not tell her where he went or what he was doing. He always made sure to let her know someone else deserved to be the object of his affection more than she did. He would make her feel like she did something wrong, and that by her actions, she caused him to do this to her.

Just like any sane human being, our survivor stood up for herself. She would tell him that she did not like him leaving her and ignoring her for days, but all this would accomplish is to start an argument. These would normally last all night and would always follow the same recipe. It would become so bizarre and confusingly repetitive that she would lose track of how it started, why it started, and what points were being made, that she eventually would be exhausted and just apologize for whatever he told her she had done wrong to cause this situation. She stopped believing in herself and stopped believing in that which was around her. She even stopped believing in her own memories. She felt completely out of touch with reality.

We've all probably heard of gaslighting, and this is where it happened to her. Eventually, she started believing the things that he told her, and when he told her she had done something wrong, even if she had no recollection of this happening she agreed and apologized. Her cognitive dissonance made her act erratically. This just served as further proof to be used against her, give a reason why she did not remember the things she apparently did wrong, as well as to convince those around her that she was indeed the problematic one in the relationship.

The narcissist is like an actor; whenever someone is around, they put on an act and appear to be extremely charming, while the other partner is used as a prop and made to look like they are incompetent and abusive in the relationship.

The narcissist weaponized her entire life, and when she saw red flags, they were explained away as part of her insecurities. When she achieved something, he took the credit for getting her there. She believed that she loved him and that her love would be all that was needed to keep the relationship alive.

It was around this time that she started to feel like she was addicted to him. If she at any time felt the relationship was in trouble, she would go through what felt to her like withdrawal symptoms. She knew that the only way to get rid of these symptoms was to repair her relationship with him and make him happy again, so he would stay with her.

This eventually led to her losing all of her friends and those close to her. This is when she started to realize that things were not as they seemed. She did what any normal person would do and tried to get her mind back first. She made an appointment with a therapist. Unfortunately, this therapist did not know much about narcissistic abuse and she didn't get much help.

She moved out of the home they shared and completely cut him and anyone else connected to him out of her life. She spent the next couple of years hiding from him and trying to rebuild her own life. During this time, she researched several ways of trauma recovery, such as neuro-linguistic programming and clinical hypnotherapy. Although her first therapist failed her, she managed to find therapy techniques that eventually allowed her to heal from this trauma.

The story I just shared with you is that of Ronia Fraser. She is now an award-winning trauma recovery coach and clinical hypnotherapist.

The Relationship Overview

At the start of the relationship, the narcissist will make you feel that you are heard, they will validate your feelings, and they will make you feel loved. They will be giving you compliments on everything, anything you do will be done just right, and the narcissist will be right there to point it out for you.

The narcissist has another trick they will use on you, especially if they feel that you did not like them during the first interaction. They will show you a wound on their soul from having a troubled childhood or a previous traumatic event, and make you feel the emotions of caring for them.

They get you to lower your guard by showering positive focus on you, while you are in this good space, and surrounded by all the positive energy they shift the focus onto themselves but they keep that energy in the atmosphere so it gets transferred to them now.

When the narcissist has ensured that they have become your world, they no longer care about keeping up this image of total adoration. And suddenly you feel that you are no longer good enough. This could happen through them directly telling it to you or a multitude of other ways.

What Is Narcissistic Abuse?

To understand narcissistic abuse better, I would like to have a look at the cycle that this type of abuse adapts. There are four stages of this abuse and I'll be exploring each of them.

Idealization Stage

This is always the first stage of the abuse and this stage starts as soon as the narcissist lays eyes on their intended victim. From the moment of meeting their victim, the narcissist will shower them with affection, compliments, adoration, and even gifts. They will try to make you believe that they immediately fell in love with you and that it was love at first sight for both of you, almost as if you were star-crossed lovers.

This first stage will start as soon as you meet, and will move along swiftly. This stage is meant to feel intense. The goal is to quickly create equally intense emotions in you, and this is why the technique used is called love bombing. You are attacked by a barrage of affection meant to disorientate you so the narcissist can lead you in the direction they want to. As soon as they realize they have this control over you, they will move onto the devaluation stage.

Devaluation Stage

Now that you love them, you don't realize it, but the first steps of your addiction to them have already started. The next step in cementing your addiction is to make you realize how much you actually need this affection. You have gotten so used to it in such a short time that you don't actually realize it until it is gone.

By starting small, the progression will feel natural and give you less reason to question it. They'll break you down bit by bit, each time progressing slightly until it went from telling you that your food doesn't taste as good as their own, to tell you that you are a failure as a person without it raising the alarm too much.

This is also where the gaslighting and breaking down occurs. When they start telling you that you did something wrong, where they get you to start questioning your memory and yourself, and where they start cutting you off from those around you.

Some signs that you are in this stage of the relationship are:

- passive-aggressiveness

- backhanded compliments

- excuses for poor behavior

- subtle criticism

- silent treatment

- mind games that seem harmless

- name-calling

- no win-situations

- lack of empathy and validation

- comparisons to others

- ridicule and humiliation

Repetition Stage

By the end of the devaluation stage, you will feel drained, depressed, anxious, and confused. The narcissist is smart enough to know that if you are kept in such an emotional stage for too long, they will lose control over you. To counteract this, they will repeat the idealization stage, but not as passionately as they did the first time.

Then, as soon as you feel that everything is okay again, they will start the devaluation stage again. This time; however, it will last slightly longer and break you down slightly more. They will push your boundaries and see how far they can go before they need to revert back to idealization again.

This is how the cycle will continue and during the devaluation stage, they will even insult your efforts and the results of it. During the idealization stage, they may give you some praise, or just not break you down.

Discard Stage

After the repetition stage has played out a few times, the cycle normally shifts to the discard stage. This stage can occur in one of two ways. Either the narcissist will cease to see a use for their victim, or the victim will realize that they are not in a healthy relationship.

When the first scenario plays out, it will feel like it came out of nowhere. The narcissist will just wake up one day and decide that this relationship is no longer beneficial to them, and eventually just end the relationship. This, however, will not be the end of their abuse. If the narcissist ends the relationship on their terms, they will try to keep control over you and use you in any way they can while they find and use their next victim.

The alternative is if the victim realizes the toxic nature of the relationship and tries to leave on their terms. This is normally the most difficult way to leave the narcissist, as they will try to keep them under their control by love bombing them again. Normally the best way to completely break free is to go completely no contact with this person.

Effects of Narcissistic Abuse

Even if you break free from narcissistic abuse, the effects of this will remain with us for quite a while. Most of these effects will start taking hold during the relationship already and before we can work to get rid of them, we need to understand them as well.

Anxiety

The good thing about anxiety is that every time you feel anxiety, you are one step closer to no longer suffering from anxiety. This is a symptom that will, over time, diminish while you are away from the cause of your anxiety, and can even be sped along with the help of a therapist.

Anxiety can show itself during the relationship already and is a result of constantly having to walk around on eggshells the entire time, as well as the dependency the narcissist forces you to develop on them.

After leaving the relationship, anxiety will present itself, especially around new people. The reason for this is that you are constantly afraid of returning to a similar situation and even slight missteps on the side of the new person will be an emotional trigger for your anxiety, whether they are actually showing signs of narcissism or not.

Anxiety can also present itself as separation anxiety. This will be similar to the so-called withdrawal symptoms you suffer from when you were away from the narcissist during the relationship and is, in fact, an extension of this.

Depression

Depression will also show itself during the relationship and especially during the devaluation stage. Even if you manage to leave the relationship during the idealization stage, these words, comments, and attacks from the narcissist will remain with you and will resurface again when the narcissist is no longer there to love bomb you. The feelings of worthlessness are often made worse because the survivor will isolate themselves from society due to their depression, making it even harder for those around them to show them their worth. If you are feeling depressed, I want you to know that this is okay, you are not doing anything wrong, and your feelings are completely valid. You are not a victim anymore, you are now a survivor, and it takes strength to survive abuse like this. You have lived through all of the worst days you've had so far, and there are so many more good days waiting for you. Do not be afraid to go at your own pace. This is how you heal, and as long as it works for you, you're doing it right.

Post-Traumatic Stress Disorder

PTSD ties in quite a bit with anxiety. The reason for this is that when you are in a situation that reminds you of the events that caused your trauma, and yes, narcissistic abuse absolutely causes you trauma, it triggers a fight-or-flight reaction within you that causes an anxiety attack. The main difference between PTSD, and anxiety is that with normal anxiety, you will feel in an almost constant state of anxiety, whereas with PTSD you will suffer from a definite anxiety attack that is only caused by an emotional trigger that reminds you of your trauma.

Loss of Sense of Self and Self-Worth

When you look into the mirror and you do not recognize the person you see looking back, you are suffering from a loss of self. This is because the narcissist has changed the way you think and see yourself during the course of the relationship. Your experiences have changed you, you now perceive the world differently.

Inability to Forgive Yourself

You could feel like you are not worthy of love because you caused the abuse or even just let it happen to yourself. You could also feel that if you had acted differently or had made more effort in the relationship, then the narcissist would not have abused you. You could be thinking that because of this part of your history, you would also mess up any future endeavors that will include your hopes and dreams.

Physical Symptoms

The stress and strain these relationships cause you could leave lasting physical symptoms, from minor headaches to migraines, body pains, and even insomnia. These occur when your body starts to realize during the relationship that something is wrong, that you are constantly in a tense state and under continuous strain from the stress. These symptoms do not always clear up when the cause for them is removed and can take a long time to be cleared up. This time is also extended if you are still suffering from anxiety, depression, and PTSD.

Cognitive Problems

When you experience trauma, your brain releases stress hormones that will affect your hippocampus region of your brain. This is the area of your brain that helps you to form your memories, to organize them, and to store them in the correct areas of your brain; it also helps to connect your memories to emotions and sensations. This is the area that causes certain smells, tastes, sounds and images to bring up old memories and to feel the emotions that you felt at the time that memory originally occurred. When these stress hormones are released on this specific area of the brain, they adversely affect it and cause issues that can last for quite a long time after the cause of the trauma has been removed. These adverse effects include difficulty with concentration and short-term memory loss.

Emotional Lability

After you have experienced these traumatic events at the hand of your abuser, it is completely normal to have mood swings or to suffer from a form of derealization. These are two coping mechanisms on the opposite side of the spectrum. If you suffer from mood swings, they will often include feelings of extreme irritability. If you suffer from derealization, then you will also feel emotionless, as if you no longer have the capacity to feel emotions, and you will also feel disconnected from the world around you. The symptoms could include:

- being unable to correctly judge how far away objects are, or what their actual size and shape may be.

- being hypervigilant of your surroundings.

- feeling as though events that happened quite recently had happened a very long time ago.

- perceiving your surroundings to appear in a way that is not normal, such as being blurry, two-dimensional, or simply cartoonish or unreal.

Signs You Are Near a Narcissist

You Experience Dissociation as a Survival Mechanism

You feel disconnected from your environment, whether it be a physical or emotional disconnection. This is a coping mechanism that your brain uses to help you lessen the blow from ongoing trauma. This can also present itself by causing you to engage in activities that will numb your mind, including becoming obsessed with or addicted to something. The obsession will help focus your mind on something else, whereas the addictive substance will cause your mind to switch off and be distracted. These will allow your mind to escape the reality around it and enhance the dissociation.

You Walk on Eggshells

To try to keep them happy and save yourself from the constant trauma, you will be extra careful with everything you say and do. This will often also move over into the rest of your life outside of the toxic relationship that causes this. Constantly being careful of your own behavior and surroundings will be your natural attempt to avoid reliving this continuous trauma, as well as minimize the occurrences of these events.

You Put Aside Your Basic Needs And Desires

The goal of the narcissist is to make themselves the center of your attention. The extent of this is that you are always thinking of their needs before you think of your own. Your drive in life will move from your own dreams and goals to looking after this person. The attention may not just be focused on their basic needs, but instead on their comfort and pleasure. What makes this even worse is that you find it increasingly difficult to please them to the point where it seems to be completely impossible.

You Develop a Pervasive Sense of Mistrust

You will soon no longer trust anyone, not even yourself. A mixture of being wronged by this person that had started to mean so much to you, and who had become the most trusted person in your life, and completely questioning your own actions and decisions in life has left you with severe trust issues. When you meet someone new, you feel that you cannot trust them at all and instead of the normal hesitancy you feel towards a new person, you are now extremely critical and completely scared of accepting the word of anyone.

You Self-Isolate

The abuser starts the isolation process, but the victim of the abuse will often continue this process by themselves. We also live in an imperfect society where victim-blaming occurs quite a lot, and this added to the friends that protect the narcissist causes the victim to feel afraid of speaking up. Instead of facing a repeat of the trauma and facing the critique and belittlement of a society that may not believe them, the victim will continue to isolate themselves thinking, that it saves them from feelings of shame.

You Self-Sabotage And Self-Destruct

The words of the narcissist will continue to ring in the mind of the victim. This is a direct result of their abuse. When pursuing their dreams and ambitions they will start to feel that they cannot accomplish them, and with the negative voice being so loud they will instead do something, even if subconsciously to get themselves out of these situations in which they are feeling unsure. This is where self-destruction comes in. The victim can try to destroy the entire life they had built which could also lead to them attempting suicide as a final act of self-destruction.

You Fear Doing What You Love And Achieving Success

Narcissists will often abuse their victims based on their own insecurities. This could become evident when they abuse their victim based on being envious of their success. Eventually, the victim will face punishment for succeeding. This reprograms the mind of the victim to associate these negative feelings and the punishment with their own success. This will cause the victim to be scared of succeeding as they are used to feeling terrible over these achievements.

You Protect Your Abuser And Even 'Gaslight' Yourself

The abuser makes their victim believe that they are completely dependent on the abuser. They also make the victim believe that they are completely in love with their abuser and that the abuser is completely in love with the victim. This causes the victim to suffer from cognitive dissonance when being abused because they find it extremely hard to accept that in a relationship where there is this much love they can be treated with cruelty and hatred. In an attempt to make sense of this situation and to diminish the effects of cognitive dissonance the victim often convinces themselves that there is no abuse.

People Doubt the Abuse Took Place

When the victim tells those around them that they are being abused, these people may not believe that the victim is indeed being abused. I want to stress here that they will believe the victim feels abused, but they will doubt whether these feelings are valid. The reason for this is that the abuser will be extremely subtle with their abuse, especially in public. They will often hide their abuse under humoristic jabs that seem to be nothing more than jokes to those looking in from the outside, but will be clear to the victim that they are in fact being broken down.

They've Started a Smear Campaign

The abuser will try to make sure everyone believes that they have done nothing wrong and that you are the one with the problematic behavior. To do this, they will attempt to get others to join in on criticizing you. They will take a scenario that happened and twist it completely so that it appears that you acted unreasonably towards them instead of the other way around. When narcissists cannot control you anymore, they will try to control those around you.

You Have Trouble Making Decisions

We've already covered this a bit, but this point deserves to not only be looked at but also to be reiterated. The absolute lack of self-esteem and negative self-image that is instilled upon the victim by the narcissist causes the victim to completely doubt their own abilities. This doubt will cause the victim to question themselves every time they make a decision. This can also be made worse if you believe that there is a problem with your memory. When the narcissist makes you believe that you said or did things that you cannot remember, or that events you vividly remember did not actually happen you could have a paralyzing fear that any decision you make could not actually be happening or that you would act incorrectly or misunderstand the decision you make yourself.

You Always Feel Like You've Done Something Wrong

This is a direct result of the narcissist refusing to accept responsibility for their own actions. When you get blamed for everything going wrong, even when you are not involved in the situation at all it causes you to feel that you are constantly doing something wrong. This feeling will also follow you out of the relationship. Eventually, whenever anything goes wrong in your life, whether you had control over it or not, you will blame yourself and believe that you must have somehow made a mistake or did something wrong that caused it.

You Have Unexplained Physical Symptoms

We've also looked at this a bit earlier, but we will be looking into this again as this is not only an effect as a result of a relationship with a narcissist but also serves as a sign to show you that you are in the presence of a narcissist. When you are in a relationship with a narcissist and find yourself in a constant state of fear and stress, your body will be the first to let you know. Your eating habits and appetite may change; some of us eat more and some of us eat less during times of distress. Your stomach is also a great indicator as you could develop medical issues such as ulcers and other gastrointestinal issues. Other than that your body will also feel fatigued due to all these issues because your mind is in a state of distress you could suffer from insomnia as well.

You Feel Restless And Unsettled

Due to the uncertain environment, you constantly find yourself in, you will constantly be on edge. You will mentally be prepared to try to de-escalate the situation or to endure a verbal and emotional assault. At the same time, you will be feeling uncertain of yourself as you can just as easily be the recipient of adoration and affection, add that to the fact that you already feel you are constantly doing something wrong, and you'll be scared that being on edge will cause you to react inappropriately and so doing be the cause of an entirely new and different conflict. All these emotions will make you feel even more on edge and uncertain.

You Don't Recognize Yourself

This is another aspect that is both an effect but also an excellent sign of being involved with a narcissist. Early on in the relationship, you may not realize exactly what is not making sense or what is different when you look in the mirror. You may not even have to look in the mirror to feel disconnected from yourself. Simply feeling that there is something missing from your life or that there is an enjoyment missing that you cannot place may be enough. The reason for this is prioritising the feelings of your abuser over your own needs, you will start giving up your social needs and hobbies to focus on the abuser and this is what will make you feel like something is slightly off with yourself.

You Have Trouble Setting Boundaries

The narcissist believes that you belong to them. You should be referring to their better judgment at all times and avail yourself to them at all times, as well as be able to prove your devotion to them at all times. To accomplish all this, they do not allow you to have any boundaries. So when you do try to put boundaries in place, no matter how healthy, the narcissist will not allow them. They will use techniques such as directly challenging these boundaries. They could also completely ignore your boundaries. The other technique they may use is to stonewall you and give you the silent treatment until you finally relent and allow them to overstep the boundary.

How The Narcissist Manipulates

We've looked at quite a bit of the relationship with a narcissist now and have a very good idea how to spot the narcissist and what their goals are, and we have an overview on how they manage to achieve this. But now I would like to take a closer look at the specific techniques they use. We know that the narcissist manipulates us and that they use love bombing and devaluation to achieve this goal, but those are very broad terms. In this section, I would like to pay closer attention to the tools that they use on us.

Lying

Narcissists lie so often and so well that it almost becomes second nature to them. They are absolute experts and their lies have no limits. Narcissists, however, will very quickly learn that a lie of omission is more effective in manipulation than a straight-out lie.

Intrude and Interrupt

When an argument ensues and emotions are running high, it's absolutely normal for anyone to interrupt another person's argument, so whenever the narcissist does this it's not frowned upon or questioned; the trick here is how they do it. The narcissist will interrupt you only in public to ensure that you are silenced and cannot make a valid point in front of others, they will then make use of this opportunity to change the narrative in their favor, so anyone looking into the situation takes their side.

This, however, is just the interrupt part of this tactic. As for the intrude part, this is where the narcissist will say and do whatever they want to, whether it is to the face of their victim or behind their back.

Deflection, Diversion, and Evasion

When they're confronted about a lie or unacceptable actions, they will use this technique to get themselves out of the crosshairs. They will possibly deflect the question or accusation onto their victim by acting enraged or wronged by it, as if the accusation hurt their feelings or was just completely ridiculous, to begin with.

They could also divert the conversation into a completely different direction and continue doing so until you can no longer remember the original issue or feel that it is less important than the new topic of the conversation. Narcissists are experts at doing this by using your own words against you.

Alternatively, they can evade the topic completely by giving a response that does not actually answer the question or accusation at all. They are also experts at this and will often use lies of omission to accomplish this goal.

Amplification

Any faults you have will be blown out of proportion. The narcissist will take your faults and amplify them and the effects thereof to make you look worse than you actually are. They will also spread the news of your shortcomings as far and wide as they can. At the same time, anything that you achieve will either be overlooked or diminished to mean almost nothing.

Emotional Blackmail

The narcissist understands that their victim requires an emotional connection and that they need validation and adoration from someone in their life. If the victim is not already in a mental state to require this, the narcissist will enforce this feeling upon the victim. Once the victim is in this mindset, the narcissist will use these feelings and emotions to blackmail the victim.

Emotional Barriers

The narcissist will attempt to control the emotions of the victim by placing barriers on what emotions they are allowed to feel under certain circumstances. This will change on the whim of the narcissist and may not always be consistent. The barriers can include both when the victim is allowed to feel positive as well as negative emotions.

Guilt Trip

This is a direct intimidation tactic. The narcissist will tell the victim that they have their life way too easy, that they are selfish and do not care about anyone or anything, or that they do not deserve everything that they have. This tactic is not only used to break the victim down, but to also make sure that they remain submissive and doubt themselves.

Inappropriate Restrictions

The narcissist will attempt to restrict the victim from actions in their everyday life that will stop them from achieving happiness, success, or anything else that they believe the victim should not be allowed to achieve. The narcissist will achieve these restrictions through their own behavior. Whether that is through emotional manipulation of the victim or that of those around the victim.

Threats

This can definitely appear as violent threats, but more often than not the narcissist will be able to get away with emotional and societal threats. The threats can include social exclusion, professional sabotage, severe restrictions, and even complete withdrawal from the narcissist, but done in such a way that the victim fears the departure of the narcissist.

Objectifying

The narcissist will use this technique to dehumanize their victim and repurpose them for their own specific needs. The narcissist will plan on their victim fulfilling this purpose and no other purpose, whether it is of a sexual nature, to be a toy for them to use for their own emotional purposes, for them to be a source of income for them or just to alleviate their boredom by playing with someone else's life. When done with skill and correctly the narcissist can so expertly dehumanize the victim to the point that the victim themselves will start sharing the feeling of the narcissist regarding themselves and their uses in life.

Shaming

This is another manipulation technique that is used to break down the victim to the point of them having feelings of inadequacy and eventual submission. This is achieved through directly insulting and causing humiliation for the victim, especially in front of other people. These can be from comments that express disappointment, contempt or disgust.

Blaming

This is another part to the aspect of the narcissist that refuses to accept responsibility for their actions. The narcissist will place the blame of all the abuse their victim suffers on the victim themselves. Their goal here is to have the victim become defensive as this will serve as proof that the victim is acting guilty, and makes it appear as if the narcissist is innocent.

Invalidation

The narcissist will try to make the victim feel that their feelings are made up or exaggerated, that the abuse never happened, and any mistreatment of the victim was unintentional as well as not severe enough to be considered abuse. The idea behind this is to further confuse the victim and question their feelings as well as their memories, in this way the narcissist will be able to not only inflict more pain on their victim, but also gain more control over them.

Silent Treatment

The goal of this technique is two-fold. It will withhold the emotional support that the victim has become dependent on, while at the same time restricting their ability to change these circumstances. In this way, the narcissist devalues the presence and opinion of the victim as it is not worthy to be heard or responded to as well as punishing them for whatever the narcissist perceived the victim had done wrong.

Negative Reinforcement

In this technique, the narcissist will almost always have a negative attitude and behavior towards the victim. They will continue to treat the victim poorly while only on rare and random occasions showing adoration or affection towards the victim in order to keep them unsure of the situation they find themselves in. The idea behind this technique is to make the victim yearn for the rare bit of positive behavior from the narcissist. When the victim yearns for this attention, the narcissist will continue to only display negative behavior and will use some positive behavior only in the rare case that the victim manages to accomplish the narcissist's impossible demands.

Positive Reinforcement

This technique works quite similar to the negative reinforcement technique with the exception that the normal behavior is that of generous positivity. The narcissist will expect that if they had been nice to the victim, it entitles them to a favor or gift from the victim, eventually, the continuous positive reinforcements will entitle the narcissist to the constant attention and time of the victim. Should the victim not avail themselves or fulfill the wishes of the narcissist, the narcissist will then take back their gifts, and withhold their emotional support and their own admiration and affection.

Gaslighting

When a narcissist gaslights the victim, they take the words and situations that the victim has found themselves in and they change the facts and twist the words so the meanings of the words and actions of the victim is changed. The goal behind this technique is to cause confusion and self-doubt in the victim so that they eventually trust the word of the narcissist over their own thoughts and memories.

Covert Aggressive Abuse

This is extremely similar to humiliation but is done a lot more subtly and in a calmer way meant to come across more as a teaching moment or as gentle advice meant to help the victim. The critique and the advice is given so regularly and in such a way that it makes the victim feel diminished and insulted while those around them see absolutely no problem with their behavior.

Playing the Victim

This is a way for the narcissist to shift blame from themselves, discredit the actual victim, as well as begin manipulation over others. The narcissist will explain that any negative or bad situation was due to the actions of others, and that their own actions were forced by someone else, or because it was the only way they felt they could react during the situation. When their actual victim tries to bring attention to their behavior and show proof that the narcissist acted poorly, the narcissist will react by claiming that they were being manipulated and misled by the victim and not the other way around.

Vilifying the Victim

This is an extremely crafty technique and will often be used at the point where the victim starts to talk out about the abuse and others start seeing the abuse for themselves. The goal of this technique is to turn the tables on the victim in the ultimate way. To not only make them appear like the aggressor but to actually get them to start being the aggressor without realizing it. This is achieved by antagonizing the victim and forcing them to feel resentment towards the narcissist shortly before the narcissist wants them to explode, and to do it in such a way that the victim does not realize that they have this feeling until they are in an emotional state where this resentment will bubble over and come bursting out. By accomplishing this, the victim is made into the unstable aggressor.

Exaggerating

Narcissists love nothing more than to exaggerate, especially when it comes to themselves. They will often overstate their abilities and importance of their roles in the lives of others. This is a manipulation technique used to get other to like them and to keep liking them. When their value is questioned, they will claim that they are irreplaceable and that they add the most value to their lives. When coupled with other manipulation techniques, the victim will often believe that what the narcissist is saying is in fact true, and will give them pause to walk away from the toxic relationship created by the narcissist.

Minimizing

This is a direct contrast of exaggeration. While the narcissist will overplay the importance of their positive traits and their imagined values, at the same time they will play down the extent of their negative traits and the effects these traits cause. They will not stop there; however, but will also downplay or deny the feelings of their victims if these negative feelings can be traced back to the narcissist as a direct cause.

Scapegoating

This is another technique used to escape responsibility for their own actions by the narcissist. The main difference in this technique is that the narcissist will pick their victim, usually this person will be within their social circle. Once the narcissist has picked their victim, they will blame everything that goes wrong on this person. In doing so, they will make this person feel inferior and small. To add insult to injury, the narcissist will manipulate the entire social circle to cut off the scapegoat and completely remove them from the social circle. This shifts the blame away from the narcissist and gives them a feeling of power over their social circle for not only being able to manipulate each and every one of them, but also to control the entire life of one of them.

Brainwashing

The narcissist already feels they are better than their victim. This is reiterated to them by the fact that they have managed to exert any amount of control over the victim. A major part of exerting this control is by brainwashing their victim into changing their own views in life to match up with those of the narcissist and that which the narcissist wants them to believe. This is achieved through intense mental and emotional pressure, as well as abuse. The victim is led to believe that their perception of the world, the people around them, and their own life is fundamentally flawed. The manipulator will use any sense of superiority that they feel they have over the victim to make the victim feel that they cannot escape and that if they want to succeed and better themselves they need to change their mindset in the way the narcissist wants them to.

Brandishing Anger

One of the best ways to control someone is by using fear. The best way to make someone fear you is by exploding on them, proving to them that you have a temper that can be dangerous and threaten them with physical violence while verbally abusing them. When this fear is instilled in a victim successfully, it can be used to condition them to do whatever it takes to not provoke this reaction from the narcissist again. It usually only takes one major blowout and only a few warnings afterward to instill this conditioning upon the victim. The trick here is that the narcissist is never actually this angry and losing their temper. This is all an act they put up to instill fear and manipulate the victim.

Intentional Vagueness

This is similar to lying by omission, the difference between the two is that lying by omission is used to entrap and deceive the victim, whereas the intentional vagueness is used to explain away their behavior and actions. The narcissist will leave their statements open to interpretation on purpose to try to distract the people whom question their actions from the actual question and matter at hand.

Lesser of Two Evils

This is another way for the narcissist to diminish their actions and try to invalidate the feelings of their victim. They will give their victim two options, both negative, but one option considerably more negative than the other.

Chapter 3:

The Realities of a Narcissistic Relationship

The Love Overview

What Does It Mean to Fall in Love With a Narcissist?

In short, falling in love with a narcissist means that someone has entered your life with the explicit goal of controlling your life, building you up, and breaking you down for nothing more than their own selfish needs. But to better understand what it means, I would like to look into the seven stages of a relationship with a narcissist from the viewpoint of the victim.

Falling in Love

This is akin to the idealization stage of the relationship. During this time, the narcissist will make an absolute effort to hide their red flags. This is the stage where they will love bomb you, compliment you, and be attentive and generous. You will feel impressed by the attention they give you.

They will convince you that you were meant to meet them. The narcissist will tell you that you possess the amazing qualities that they do not and that it is these exact qualities of you that attracted them, like two puzzle pieces you were made to complete each other.

The Twist

When you are used to this level of adoration and love that the narcissist has been showering upon you, you start to notice that they become a bit distracted. The stolen moments that once made you feel like you two are the only two people in existence now feel almost forced, almost as if they are getting bored.

The Confusion

The first two stages happened so fast that you are still trying to figure out what exactly happened. You will find yourself in a very negative mindset dealing with feelings of rejection and betrayal, depression and anger, missing the narcissist but feeling absolutely furious at them. At this moment you also feel anger at yourself for not realizing that this relationship was too good to be true, but at the same time you miss the narcissist and their love bombing and all you want to do is get back to that first stage of falling in love.

Don't Try to Talk It Out

Your first reaction will be to try to clear up the confusion. To have an open and honest conversation, to try to find out what went wrong. But if you ask them why they are acting strangely towards you they feel taken aback, they get angry and will explode at you, or just ignore you for trying to blame everything on them. This reaction will hurt you so much that eventually, you apologize for everything they say you did wrong.

They Don't Care

They've accepted you back, they may even have been nice to you again and showed some affection, but it doesn't last. Soon they are distant again, they are showing you little to no affection, and seem to be unhappy or angry whenever you are around. You start wondering if you did something wrong again, and you decide that you must have. You try apologizing again, but this time it's not good enough. So you start looking for ways to make them happy.

Alone Again

One of two things finally happens. The first is that the narcissist finally gets bored of you. You don't make them happy anymore. And with that, they will walk out of your life. You will feel like you completely failed them. You will feel like a failure and as if you are worthless. It hurts even more that they couldn't see how much you were hurting, or maybe they just didn't care anymore.

The second thing that could happen is that you realize that it is not you, and the way they are treating you is not the right way. You take a long hard look at your situation and begin to realize what has been going on the entire time, so you decide to walk away from it. But when you do, they will probably try to contact you and win you back. They try to make you feel guilty for leaving them and make you think that you are the one that just used them and then threw them away.

Acceptance

Finally, you gain some new perspective on the relationship and you start to see how you were abused. You start to realize how erratic their behavior and standards for you were, and you finally start to accept that it was not you that caused the negativity in them and in the relationship. It was them. This is when your relationship with the narcissist truly starts coming to an end and your healing beings.

Why Do You Fall in Love With a Narcissist?

By now you may be wondering why anyone would ever fall in love with a narcissist. Even without researching NPD we know that having any type of relationship with a narcissist is bad news for us. So why if we know this do some people still fall in love, and stay in love with a narcissist, especially once they know this person is a narcissist? There are a few reasons actually, let's look at them.

Positive Qualities

Although we have so far focused on the negative characteristics of the narcissist, the truth of the matter is that narcissists do also possess qualities that can be seen as positive. These will be qualities like intelligence, having an amazing sense of humor, fun-loving, well-mannered and so many more that I cannot possibly list all of them. These traits make it a lot easier to fall in love with a narcissist, especially since they appear to be more of a nice person than a narcissist usually does.

Repeating Our Trauma

When someone grows up with authority figures that are narcissists it is not uncommon for them to be attracted to narcissists without realizing it. The reason for this is that their subconscious is attempting to finally get the love and validation that was lacking from their childhood. When they meet a narcissist, the pattern can feel so familiar to them that it is even easier for them to fall into it without even realizing that they are doing it or why. Most often, this person does not get the outcome they desire, instead they go through the same pain again and old wounds can also be re-opened.

They're Like a Drug

When a narcissist is especially charming, they make you completely desire a relationship with them. They can make you feel like you are a special treasure that they have decided to collect, and the feeling you get from being unique to them, from being chosen over everyone else can be almost addictive right from the start. These charmers, however, are similar to a drug in another way as well. When they eventually discard you and no longer find you interesting, the rejection and end of the relationship is also a lot more intense.

Narcissists Are Not All the Same

As I have mentioned before, narcissists exist on a spectrum, one we are all a part of as we all possess some narcissistic traits. This also means that there are narcissists on this spectrum that can be seen as higher functioning individuals. These narcissists have learned how to reign in their emotions and narcissistic tendencies. They may be less inclined to abuse people and may be able to remain in a healthy relationship much longer than other narcissists. At the same time, there are also narcissists on the spectrum that are seen as lower functioning. These are more inclined to be abusive and their relationships will turn toxic much faster than that of others.

They Don't Know Until It Is Too Late

When you meet a narcissist, it is not always immediately apparent, and unfortunately, by the time the red flags start popping up it could already be too late. You could think that you're dealing with a normal person that has a few personality traits you like, spend some time with them, get to know them better and eventually fall in love. By the time the red flags start showing themselves to you, it may already be too late and you could simply already be hooked.

Signs and Attractions

Telltale Signs You Are in Love With a Narcissist

Charming but for Their Good

We've established it quite well by now that the narcissist will start by charming you. Here I would like to point out that gradually this charm will diminish. Charm will become only a tool used to get what they want, whether from you or someone else. You may notice that your partner can be quite charming when negotiating a price for something they want to purchase, or to a contractor they want to work faster, or their boss when they want a promotion, yet when they do not see the benefit in being charming to someone they will be completely indifferent or even rude. When the charm is not natural, it may be just an act.

Gratification Required at the Moment

We've already covered that the narcissist will require you to put their needs in front of yours, and this is the same idea. When a narcissist sends you a message and you don't reply immediately, this could lead them to go off on you. The next time someone that you suspect may be a narcissist asks you for something, try telling them "no" and see how they react. They may explode in anger, or just simply ignore you and decide to do it, regardless.

Entitlement Is Their Habit

The narcissist normally believes that they are superior to others, and thus they should be treated so. They expect that their needs and desires should be met without hesitation while they will give nothing back. This is where the saying "Watch how your partner behaves towards the waiting staff and you'll know everything you need to about them." If someone is constantly rude to the wait staff, criticizing and humiliating them, and refuse to tip them, then you may have just caught a narcissist.

Loves to Talk About Oneself

Me-me-me-me. That is all a narcissist talks about. When they enter a conversation, they will change the topic to themselves, their day, their dreams, their accomplishments, their fears. When someone tells a personal story, the narcissist will always have a story of their own, and this story will always make them seem just a bit better than the previous person. The easiest way to establish this is to keep an eye on your conversations. Do they actually listen to you and share your conversation, or do they immediately change it and make it all about them?

Lacks Reliability

The narcissist will always try to do what serves them the best. In one situation, making a promise of helping someone will serve them in making them look charming, generous, and good-hearted. When that person, however, requests to promise to be fulfilled, the narcissist will decide again what is best for themselves. Helping this person, or going out for drinks with someone that they could charm into paying for them? This is their lack of reliability and where it comes from, narcissists will have a difficult time fulfilling their promises, or even keeping appointments they had. It's also easy to spot. How many times have the narcissist offered to help you with something or you asked them to help, and they actually did it, instead of something very important coming up?

No Commitment

A narcissist may not realize it themselves, but they are horrible at making and keeping their commitments. They will only be reliable as long as it suits them, and this may end very quickly into a relationship or may last until marriage. They also find it much easier to walk away from situations like these. Think of your partner's friends and work. How long does your partner last at a job before they need to find a new one?

Boundary Violator

The narcissist will break any boundary that stands in the way of them getting what they want. Whether that is your emotional boundaries or actual rules and regulations around them. That person that moves the reserved sign in the restaurant because it's on the table they prefer, that person that finds a way to jump the queue because they are in a hurry. To see if your partner does this, just look at their driving. A narcissist will believe the speed limit is nothing more than a suggestion for the lesser people, while not wearing their safety belt.

Constantly Put Others Down

A narcissist loves to feel bigger, better, more important, and more powerful than everyone else. Sometimes to do this, they need to put others down and find flaws in those people. You will be one of the main victims of this behavior, and this will be where you find the sign. If you find that your thoughts have changed quite a bit during your relationship and that you suddenly do not believe in your own abilities or feel that you do not possess most things in your life then you have most probably already started suffering from abuse by a narcissist.

Sweeps You off Your Feet at First

We already understand love bombing and how the narcissist will use compliments and gifts to make us feel incredibly special. But at the same time, the narcissist will already be building themselves up. They will show themselves as extremely charming, successful, well put together and just an overall amazing catch, they will make us feel as if we are so lucky to have gotten someone like them, while making us think that they think the world of us. This is quite easy to spot when you know about it. When someone starts the relationship and gives you an excessive amount of gifts and compliments, it is unnatural. Yes, at the start of every relationship, these things will be more common, but if that is almost entirely your relationship, you are being love bombed.

Loses Interest Once the Chase Is Over

Once the narcissist is sure that they have you, the change will come quite fast. Their behavior towards you will suddenly change. The gifts will stop, the constant compliments will be gone, the constant texts from when you wake up until late at night will be less frequent. And if you do comment on this, you will be met with only negative emotions. Try telling your partner that you miss all the extra attention you used to get and see how they react.

Says All of Their Exes Were "Crazy"

What are the chances that every person that they dated was "crazy," "psycho," and "stalkerish," How could someone meet the same type of person repeatedly and not start seeing the signs from early on? Don't worry, the narcissist will have an explanation for it. They will also make it clear that you are their first partner that isn't "crazy." Try asking your partner about their exes, and see if they can list any that were sane according to them.

Uses Your Deepest Insecurities Against You

During the initial phase, when you are getting to know the narcissist, they will remember every insecurity and fear you tell them about, including your past trauma. These will later be used against you again. If you have told them that a certain part of your body makes you feel insecure, they will use it against you and constantly bring it up. Does your partner keep reminding you of your insecurities or using them to get you not to do something? Like using your fear of talking too much to get you to say less when you are in a social situation or to explain why they are in a foul mood when you are alone?

Constantly Reminds You That They Have Other Options

The narcissist is better than you, and is doing you a favor by being with you. They don't need you and they have lines of people begging to be with them. They constantly have potential partners approaching them on social media, and they have multiple offers at work every single day. You should count yourself lucky they are still wasting their time with you. Or so they would have you think. These are the thoughts the narcissist will place in your mind, and often these words are spoken out loud and directly. Has your partner ever said this or make you felt like this?

What Attracts Narcissists to You?

Forgiving

To allow them to continue the narcissistic abuse, they will require you to constantly forgive them, which is why this is a major trait that will draw a narcissist to you. They will also change your belief on forgiveness. The acts you previously thought would be unforgivable will become acts you forgive on a regular basis.

Brokenness

A narcissist will look for someone with past trauma. They will use this trauma to more easily manipulate your feelings towards them and to establish themselves in your life. If you had, for example, an absent parent that was never there for you, the narcissist will take on this role and aspects of it in order to give you the feelings that you felt you missed out on. This is a very easy way to have you feel like you need them.

Empathy

An empath is a person that will be more prone to show kindness and to see the situation from another person's point of view. This is amazing for the narcissist because they will be able to play the victim even after abusing the narcissist and then have their victim end up feeling sorry for them and consoling them.

Loyal

A narcissist wants you to focus all your attention on them, to isolate you from everyone around you, and to have your energy all focused only on them. They also want you to remain at their side, even if they abuse you and treat you poorly. A person with a loyal nature is already halfway there at the start and makes reaching their goal much easier.

Low Self-Esteem

When you have low self-esteem, it is easier for the narcissist to make you feel good during their love bombing attempts, and when they want to break you down later it will also be quite easy for them. They find the manipulation of someone with lower self-esteem in either direction to be easier to do and their goal faster to achieve.

Overly Accommodating

The narcissist wants nothing more to use you, to have you sacrifice your own self in favor of theirs. When they meet someone who is already over accommodating, it is even easier to get them to give up the rest of themselves to the narcissist.

Overly Responsible

Think closely about what a responsible person will do. When you go on a trip this person will make sure that everything is packed, everyone has their visas and plane tickets, there are snacks and something to drink, and that everything is ready. This is what the narcissist wants, because it means that you will constantly focus on their needs and ensure that they have everything they need to do. Eventually you will go from asking them if they are packed, to actually packing for them.

Self-Sacrificing

This is probably the trait that most attracts a narcissist. If you are willing to sacrifice yourself and your own needs at the beginning of the relationship already, almost all of their work is already done and they can enjoy having you at their control much sooner.

Why People Are Attracted to Narcissists

We've looked at what we find attractive in narcissists and what they find attractive in us, now it's time to look at why we are attracted to them in the first place, not just the traits they possess that they use to pull us in, but the reaction of our subconscious that makes us want to be there and why.

There Are No Coincidences

If you entered a relationship with a narcissist, it is because they wanted you to. They chose you and used every trick they could until they could convince you that they are what you want. If you enter a relationship with a narcissist more than once; however, it may be because there is a subconscious part of you looking for them. This is often driven by self-destructive behavior and could stem from past trauma.

You Experienced Narcissistic Abuse as a Child

Childhood is the stage of our life in which our personality and ideas are formed. If during this time we are formed to please a narcissist, it will stick with us during our adulthood. A narcissist will find you their perfect prey because you have already been trained, they just need to fine tune you.

You Have Low Self-Esteem

For someone with low self-esteem, a toxic relationship can almost feel symbiotic. The narcissist will feed on your low self-esteem and find it easier to bend you to their will, but for the person with low self-esteem, it could feel like the narcissist is their polar opposite. They are confident, capable, and in control, and these traits could make it feel like they are enriching the quality of your life.

You Have Codependent Tendencies

Someone with codependent tendencies will find it difficult to be alone, and they will have an almost obsessive need to find a partner. This will mean that their standards for a partner will lower with time, as they attempt to find someone else. They will also do more and try to keep their partner even after quite more severe abuse than others normally will.

You're Naïve

Naïve people are easier to manipulate because they do not necessarily understand or catch on to the underlying motives of the narcissist's action. This allows them to more clearly and directly manipulate the naïve person without much difficulty. When a narcissist sees someone is very naïve, they will see them as a very easy target and this makes a naïve person more prone to being targeted, and because of their nature they will easily believe that this narcissist is different than all the others they have encountered, leading them to fall into the same relationship trap again.

Narcissistic Behavior Feels Normal to You

This is very similar to someone that grew up with narcissistic abuse, but the difference here is that they may not have been the target of the abuse or suffered it during childhood. This may be someone that grew up in close proximity to a narcissist or had interactions with a series of narcissists throughout their adult lives, eventually, their behavior seems normal. This would mean that the person will not see problems with the behavior of narcissists and enter relationships with narcissists more frequently.

You Don't Value Your Own Needs and Feelings

When someone is predisposed to this kind of behavior, the narcissist will be more attracted to them. Getting someone to the point of ignoring their own needs and feelings is a goal for narcissists, when this goal is achieved already the narcissist can reap the rewards, and it also makes it easier to over-step on other boundaries. This does make this person more attractive to narcissists and more prone to being targeted.

You Have an Unfulfilled Need for Approval and Emotional Connection

This is another trait that makes you more attractive to narcissists and prone to be the repeated target of narcissists. A person that has this unfulfilled need will attempt to receive approval and an emotional connection from anyone at the moment they meet them. The narcissist will see this and realize that they will be able to get this person to work even harder than others to fulfill this need. At the same, time this person will be more susceptible to the initial love bombing of a narcissist, to the point where it gets the better of their logical thinking.

You Feel Worthless or Unlovable

This is a result of low self-esteem but it also stands very much on its own. When you feel like you are not good enough to be loved, but someone does make you feel that you are loved, then you may find it even harder than others to get away from these situations. This also makes you more prone to falling victim in the future because the love bombing and later fear of finding another person to love you will also take over from your normal logical senses.

I would like to end this chapter with a thought and a quote for you.

Narcissists are everywhere in this ripe age of self-love, which amazes me because so much in life would seem to foster humility.
—Dean Koontz

Chapter 4:

Step 1—Recognizing The

Abuse

Recognizing the Abusive Situation Overview

What Is An Abusive Relationship?

An abusive relationship is when one partner uses potentially trauma inducing behavior to maintain control over the other partner. This behavior can include physical violence, threats of physical violence, and emotional and mental manipulation. The control could emotional, physical, sexual, or financial. A Canadian study in 2020 found that women are more prone to being the victims of an abusive relationship where 35% of all women had experienced emotional childhood abuse, a total of 43% of women has endured any type of abuse as a child or adolescent, and finally, that between 2015 and 2020, 39% of women had endured abuse in a relationship.

Why You Should Recognize the Abusive Situation

You cannot leave the relationship unless you recognize that it is abusive. And even if you do leave or in some cases are forced out of the situation by the abuser as part of their abuse, you cannot heal your trauma unless you recognize that this situation was indeed abusive towards you. There are also a few other positive effects of recognizing that this behavior is indeed abusive that we will look at right now.

You Will Stop Blaming Yourself

Part of the abuse will be that the abuser will shift the blame onto you. They will make you believe that you made them angry enough to abuse you. You acted inappropriately enough to justify their actions. And that it is your fault that you have been isolated. However, when you recognize that you are in an abusive relationship, you will be able to see that your actions were not the cause of the abuse, but instead that your actions were either completely normal or a result of the abuse.

Your Stress Will Reduce

Instead of being tensed up and stressed about what you have been doing wrong, or being scared to do something else wrong without realizing it you will now start to understand that you are not in fact acting incorrectly in any way to justify these actions taken against you. This will help to alleviate your stress, as you no longer need to be on constant guard.

You Will Start Seeing the Abuser for They Are

Now that you realize that this person is abusing you, their actions and motivation behind this will become clearer. You will start to understand what their actual feelings towards you and those around them are. Their goals become clearer to you and the aspects of their personality that have been hidden until this point or that you were led to believe you are imagining will now become undoubtedly clear.

The Tactics of the Abuser Will Become Clearer

Realizing that there is abuse will also show the method of abuse to you clearly. When you know that someone is actively trying to make you feel mentally unstable you will not only look back at the time you have spent feeling unsure of your mental health, you will also look at what caused these feelings within you, and notice it more going forward. This will apply to all the forms of abuse you have become aware of and will stick out like a sore thumb to you. You will have that "aha" moment of understanding what the actual intent of their actions has been.

Your Mind Will Feel More at Peace

You will no longer be wondering about your own mental health or questioning your memory. You will no longer be neglecting your own needs, especially your mental health needs, and all of this will cause you to be able to take a mental breather. Your mind will no longer be constantly racing to anticipate their needs, to over-analyze your own actions. Think of it as your mind finally reaching the finish line after a marathon in which it had to continuously juggle feral cats.

You Are a Step Away From Saving Yourself

Knowing that you are in an abusive relationship means that you will be ready to get out of the relationship and heal. This can save your life not just physically from your abuser, but also from your own mental health. A major side effect of abuse is depression and we all know the unfortunate end that depression can lead us to. But if you understand the situation was abusive, it does have the possibility of saving you from both of these possible outcomes.

You Will Become More Productive

During the relationship, you will constantly be focusing your energy on the abuser and their needs. When you realize that this is a form of abuse you are enduring, you will instinctively move away from this. When you do this, you suddenly have a lot of energy available to you that you can redirect into other aspects of your life, such as self-care and work. With all the extra energy you are suddenly directing at these aspects, you will be able to achieve your goals in them more easily and spend more time on these aspects.

You Will Sleep Better

With the combination of having more mental energy and clarity as well as relieving stress and tension in your body, you will find that it is not only easier to fall asleep, but that you enter a deeper state of sleep and feel more rested after sleep.

You Will Begin to Think of Solutions

With clarity of mind, extra energy, and realization of the situation, you will find yourself coming up with solutions of how to counteract the abuse as well as how to get away from it completely.

The Details

Why It Is Hard to Leave an Abusive Relationship

We know that the correct response to an abusive relationship is to leave it. There is usually nothing we want to do more than leave. But it is not as easy as just walking out, and to understand this completely, we need to look at the reasons behind why it is so difficult to get away.

Society Normalizes Unhealthy Behavior

Think about reality shows for a moment. The actions and behaviors of the cast are usually absolutely erratic and unhealthy, usually made even worse by producers and directors encouraging the cast to act out even more in order to make the show more interesting and intriguing for viewers. Unfortunately, this makes this behavior seem more normal and common than it should be. This behavior can also be encouraged by social media and religion, where certain behaviors and social hierarchy in social situations are encouraged. This makes it hard to not only leave but also seek help as the victim could feel that they would not get any support and that people that hear about their story may either not find any issues with the abuser's behavior or even take their side.

Emotional Abuse Destroys Your Self-Esteem

When your self-esteem is destroyed, you may not believe that you have the strength or ability to leave the relationship and survive on your own. This is not a coincidence, the abuser enforces these feelings on purpose to ensure that the victim is more hesitant and less likely to leave the situation.

The Cycle of Abuse

Abuse goes through a cycle, and as we have already established, this cycle includes a phase in which the abuser shows affection and adoration to their victim after a session of abuse. This is a tactic to not only backtrack after they have realized that they have reached the current extreme boundary. This period of love makes the victim feel that the abuse is not a constant and that it was only a rough patch in the relationship. This also makes the victim hesitant to leave as they may be back in this phase of being love bombed and be led to believe that the abuser has changed their abusive ways.

It Feels Dangerous to Leave

One of the ways of control is for the abuser to tell the victim that they will regret leaving them. This can be a threat of physical violence as well as a threat to destroy the victim's life. The problem here is that studies have found that a woman is 70 times more likely to be murdered in the weeks after the break-up than at any time during the relationship. This does scare the victim, especially if the abuser has had violent outburst regardless of whether they have included physical violence or not. The victim can be scared that the threat will be followed upon at any time.

Hard to Escape the Cycle of Control

Once a narcissist has found out how to control and manipulate you, they will use this against you forever. Part of their abuse also conditions and prepares the victim for future manipulations. This is why, on average, a victim will attempt to leave and actually break up the relationship seven times before they finally leave it for good. Often times when the victim will try to break up with their abuser, the abuser will either try to wear down their victims by constant harassment and promises of changing. Alternatively, they will use threats and further abuse to force the victim to return to them.

Society Perpetuates a Ride-or-Die Mindset

We have constant pressure from society to be loyal to a fault. We are told that we should not be giving up on relationships without trying to repair them, regardless of the reasons for ending them. This will often pressure a person to either stay in this relationship longer or return to it after they have left, as they could be seen as the wrong one in the relationship for leaving without trying everything.

Feel Responsible for Their Partner

This is a direct side effect of gaslighting and blame shifting. The victim becomes so used to bearing all the responsibility in the relationship that they feel any negative emotions or events the abuser has to endure after the end of the relationship is still their responsibility as it is a direct result of their actions.

Hope That Things Might Change

The abuser will make their victim believe that they will change their ways because they either regret their actions or because they are simply just going through a bad time of their life. As the saying goes; "a leopard cannot change its spots." The abuser will not change their behavior, they will simply act lovingly for a period of time to lull the victim back into a false sense of safety before they return to their abusive ways again. Unfortunately, they are expert liars and manipulators and will be able to convince their victim that they have the capability to change.

There is Social Pressure to Be in a Perfect Relationship

In a time where we are heavily influenced by social media, we are almost constantly bombarded by the idea of a perfect relationship. This is reinforced by influencers and normal people alike on social media, where they are giving the image of being in the perfect relationship. We do not like to admit our faults, whether a narcissist or not, and this is reflected on our social media where we only make posts about our happy and good moments, but almost never about our dark times, our fights or disagreements. There is also a cultural and religious aspect to this. In many cultures and religions, it is frowned upon for the relationship to not succeed as well as having a partner that is unhappy.

Fear of How Others Will React

With the unreasonable expectations of society as well as the ridiculous amount of victim shaming and victim blaming we endure, victims of abuse may be scared that if others find out that they have been abused, the reaction will be negative. Whether this reaction is judging the victim for "allowing this to happen" or enduring it so long, or because they will be pitied and treated differently due to this, the effects are the same. The victim will feel guilty or embarrassed.

They Share a Life Together

During the course of any relationship, you start to work on your life together. Whether you have actually shared finances and made large purchases together, whether they share social circles, and whether they have started a family together through marriage, children and pets. This connection to each other will make the victim feel that they are dependent on each other and that they are responsible for these aspects together. This is also another reason why they feel they need to work on the relationship and save it to protect these aspects of their shared lives.

Recognizing the Different Types of Narcissistic Relationship Abuse

There are multiple different types of abuse that can be exercised upon the victim. These are: physical abuse, sexual abuse, emotional abuse, and financial abuse. We will now look into these types of abuse and the signs of them.

Signs of Physical Abuse

This is when the abuser does physical harm to you. This is the most commonly known and talked about abuse in society at the moment. Physical abuse will often start out small, and will immediately be followed up by an apology. The next time it happens, there will be no immediate apology, but rather a lesser sincere apology a while later. From here on out, the physical abuse will become more aggressive and more intense with the apologies becoming less sincere and further in between to the point where they are replaced with accusations and blame.

Here are a few examples of physical abuse:

- Causing physical harm to you by slapping, punching, biting, etc.

- Denying fulfillment of your basic needs

- Damaging your possessions.

- Threatening you with further physical abuse.

- Physically restricting you from leaving.

- Forcing you out of the car in strange places and leaving you there.

- Driving in a manner to instill fear in you.

- Forcing you to consume substances.

Signs of Sexual Abuse

This can perhaps be the most sensitive topic in this book. This is because sexual activity and intimacy are seen as an extremely personal topic and not appropriate for general conversation. There is also the misconception that your partner cannot sexually assault you, and that men cannot be sexually assaulted, both of which are untrue. The goal of sexual assault is to control the sexual activities of the victim.

Here are a few examples of sexual abuse:

- Determine what you are allowed to wear and what you are not allowed to wear as well as when.

- Force you to engage in sexual activity.

- Give you a sexually transmitted disease against your will and without your knowledge.

- Place you under the influence of substance without your knowledge or forcefully in order to have sex with you.

- Ensure that a pregnancy takes place in the relationship against your wishes.

- Force you to view pornographic material.

Signs of Emotional Abuse

This is the type of abuse we have mostly been covering here, as narcissists will mostly engage in emotional abuse as this is what they will feed on. The goal of emotional abuse is to control the victim, as this gives the narcissist a sense of power and makes them feel good.

Here are a few examples of emotional abuse:

- name-calling

- constant criticism

- intentionally embarrassing you

- threatening you

- using your children against you

- threatening to hurt your children or your pets

- acting like everything is your fault

- isolating you from friends or family

- having affairs with other partners or provocative behavior with others

- making you feel guilty

Signs of Financial Abuse

Financial abuse is when the abuser uses your own finances or financial situation to exert control over you. Most often, this will mean that you will not be allowed to make your own financial decisions, they will make it for you. They will also ensure that they benefit from your finances while you personally struggle with this.

- Restricting your spending and the amount of money you have access to.

- Having your salary paid into their account.

- Withholding your access to your bank account or shared accounts.

- Limiting your ability to generate an income.

- Preventing you from making an income by restricting your access to travel.

- Jeopardizing your source of income by having you dismissed or suspended.

- limiting or restricting your access to the financial support you are entitled to.

- Using your personal information to obtain loans without your permission.

- Using your funds without your knowledge or permission.

Refusing you access to funds for basic needs.

Spending funds on themselves while restricting you from doing so.

Spending money on you with the expectation that you will reciprocate.

Using your financial circumstances to exert control over you.

Chapter 5:

Step 2—Setting Boundaries and Leaving

The Boundaries Overview

What Are Boundaries?

Unlike physical boundaries such as fences, the boundaries we will be dealing with here are ever changing. They do, however, play a similar role. The idea is to keep yourself safe from outside dangers. These dangers could be physical, mental, or emotional.

Importance of Setting Boundaries in Narcissistic Abuse

When you have healthy boundaries in your relationship, you will be able to maintain control over your own life in any situation as well as be protected from most attempts at abuse. Healthy boundaries can also give you a sense of independence. This way, connections made with others will be both healthy and positive. We will be looking into the importance of healthy boundaries in this section.

Protecting Emotional Space

Emotional boundaries allow you to draw the line at the actions of others, they will not be able to take any actions that will negatively impact your emotional well-being. This will be your safety mechanism that allows you to not let yourself be impacted and to see their true motives.

Protecting Physical Space

Physical boundaries can be extended to both your actual space around you, as well as your own body. You will be determining what level of physical contact you are comfortable with and allow others to engage in. When you extend your boundaries to your personal spaces, you will determine who is allowed into them and the actions they are allowed to take in this space. Separating your thoughts, feelings, and needs from those of others.

Not Feeling Guilty About or Responsible for the Happiness of Others

This does tie in with the previous point. Even though you may have let them down by enforcing your own boundaries, but this is another boundary you will need to set in place. It is not your responsibility to ensure that others are happy and content in their life. You are welcome to help out in a way that is healthy to you, but should not sacrifice your own happiness to ensure happiness for another person.

If you have set healthy boundaries in place and ensured that your relationships do not cross these boundaries you will find that you are actually closer to these people and will get more out of these relationships, these relationships may even make you feel more fulfilled and useful than relationships in which you lose yourself.

Protecting Your Valuable Time

By setting boundaries, you may find you can safeguard your time so that you have more of it to spend on things you value and things you need to do and with people you feel good around.

I've touched on this earlier, but the boundary of time does not just extend to the time used to help someone. It could also be used to set boundaries in time spent with anyone, and ensure that you have alone time. This can also be used to set boundaries in place to ensure that you do not spend too much time alone, thus prohibiting yourself from self-isolating again. It also ensures you have a strong sense of identity.

When your needs are taken care of, you have a greater ability to assist others to meet their needs. You will feel more fulfilled and more energized when you are well rested, fed, and feeling accomplished. This is why it's important to prioritize your needs.

Preventing Future Conflicts

With your boundaries in place, those around you will know where they can go and where they are not welcomed. When these are in place and someone oversteps in the future, you can gently remind them about your boundaries and they will most often apologize and step back. If they do not respect this boundary, you will also know who you are dealing with. This will help to prevent unnecessary conflicts that may arise, and assist you in knowing who will respect your boundaries and who will not.

Developing Independence

When you have boundaries on not only your emotions, social interactions, personal space, and finances, you will have parts of yourself for which you are solely responsible. This will allow you to feel and actually be fully independent. When you have this independence, it is harder for someone to break down your self-confidence and control you.

The Types of Boundaries

Physical Boundaries

These are the boundaries that are in place regarding your body, your home, your workspace, and your personal possessions. This can also include your rest cycle as well as what and when you eat and drink. Your rest cycle will not just include your sleep, but also when you just need to take a break from an activity or social situation.

These are a few of the questions you can ask yourself in order to set up healthy physical boundaries;

- "What are my current energy levels, do I need to sit down for a few minutes now?"

- "Is the way I am being touched acceptable to me?"

- "What level of touching am I comfortable with?"

- "Who are the people that I feel comfortable being touched by?"

- "Who do I trust to give me input on a healthy diet?"

- "How will I make sure that I get enough rest?"

Emotional Boundaries

When you set your emotional boundaries, you basically allocate how much emotional energy you reserve for your own needs, and how much emotional energy you are willing to allocate to other people around you. This needs to be a healthy amount of energy on both sides.

You cannot solely focus on yourself as this will be effective in isolating yourself. You also cannot spend too much energy on others as this will cause you to neglect yourself again.

These are a few questions to consider when setting emotional boundaries:

- "If I share my emotions with you, will you criticize me, or respond in a respectful manner?"

- "How can I respectfully tell someone that I do not have the emotional capacity to assist them at the moment, but that I will assist them when I do have the capacity to do so?"

- "How can I share my emotional concerns with someone without infringing on their emotional boundaries?"

- "Can I engage in a conversation regarding this topic at the moment or should I ask to have this conversation at another time?"

Sexual Boundaries

Healthy sexual boundaries allow you to safely explore and enjoy your sexuality and sex life. It is also intended for you to be able to communicate your boundaries to your sexual apartment in order to ensure that you are protected and safe at all times.

These are a few points that should form part of sexual boundaries;

- Always ensure that you both give and receive consent.

- Discuss your interests and dislikes beforehand.

- Ensure that the experience is as safe as requested by either party.

- Ensure that both parties are aware of the possibility of pregnancy and the use of contraceptives.

- Ensure that both parties have the option and ability to stop any activity that they are uncomfortable with at any time.

- Ensure that the privacy of both parties is protected at all times.

How to Leave an Abusive Relationship

Step 1: Prepare Yourself Emotionally

The abuse during your relationship was aimed at destroying your mental health, confidence, and self-esteem. When you want to leave the relationship, this breakdown of your mental health will be one of your major obstacles. To combat this, you will need to retrain your mind to be prepared for this.

Give Words to Your Experience

You need to be able to look back upon your abuse and document it, looking at the first evidence of abuse and the latest experience of the abuse you had. Look at the way these experiences had made you feel, what they had done to make you feel like this, and what your actions leading up to and immediately afterward were. Make sure that you write all of this down. This will help you to make sense of this and when you are ready to share this information with a third party such as a friend or therapist, they can use this information to validate your experiences.

Keep a Journal

The best way to understand your own experiences is to write them down. Keep a journal where you have a record of the abuse, dates, times, and locations where it happened. Keep a record of what your abuser did, what they said, and how it made you feel. When you have all this information recorded and you find yourself unsure whether or not you want to go through with walking away from this situation, you can reread these records to remind yourself of why you felt like this in the first place. This will help to strengthen your resolve and to remind you why you do not want to go back after you left.

Realize Your Partner Won't Change

You need to start understanding that you do not have the ability to completely change an entire person. You may be able to assist them in improving some parts of their traits, provided they are willing to change that and work with you. A narcissist will not be prepared to do so, but will attempt to fool you into thinking that they did, and will revert to their old ways very quickly.

Be Ready to Grieve

Ensure that you do not just prepare yourself to leave, but that you are also prepared to miss them, to feel sorrow over the end of the relationship, and to even feel sorry for them. Remind yourself during this time that you have the ability to survive on your own, reread your journal and strengthen your resolve in the decision you've made.

Step 2: Lay the Groundwork

Many people feel fear during this time, especially since they have been threatened with violence and death. For this reason, you will need to plan your escape before you leave. You need to be prepared to be able to get out under dire circumstances and quite quickly.

Pack Your Bags

Get everything that is important, such as legal documentation and banking documents, as well as some clothing and other bits and pieces that will be essential after you left the situation. Be sure that you remove these belongings in a very subtle way so the abuser does not realize that they are missing. Give these items to someone you can trust so the abuser does not find them by accident.

Find a Support System

This will be a difficult and potentially dangerous time for you. During this time, you will need as much assistance as you can get in a variety of ways. Have friends that are willing to help you emotionally and physically by listening and helping you pack and leave when the time comes. You can also look into seeing a therapist who can assist you with your emotional trauma and working through the feelings and manipulation that will pop up during this time.

Find a Secure Means of Seeking Help

Have your way planned out in such a way that you are as safe as can be. Try to make sure that you can leave when the abuser is not at home. This is normally the safest way. Alternatively, be sure that you have other people present when you plan on leaving as they are less likely to become physically violent if another person or multiple people are present. You can also approach your local police station and request a police officer as assistance when you leave, and explain to them that you believe your life may be in danger.

Figure Out Where You'll Go

This is a vital part of the plan. Make sure you have somewhere to go, whether it is a place of your own, a friend's place, or even just a shelter. If you simply leave and end up on the street, it will be easier for the abuser to entice you back into their environment and it may also be unsafe for you as it may make you easier to be found by the abuser or others with malicious intent.

Be Alert to Your Partner's Changes in Behavior

No matter how careful you are, your partner may realize that you are acting differently or that some things are missing. When they do, they might not immediately become aggressive but could instead suddenly become the dream partner again. This will make you question whether you are making the correct choice and will keep you in the situation longer. Be on the lookout for such changes and get out immediately if you do suspect that they may know in any way.

Establish Emergency Funds or Credit

If you have been the victim of an abusive relationship, there is a very good chance that the narcissist has exercised some sort of financial abuse upon you. This could mean that when you leave the relationship, you may not have finances available to you or they might have access to your finances that you are unaware of and can cut you off to try and force you back into their hold. To prepare for this, make sure that you have some emergency cash hidden away somewhere safe where the abuser cannot find it, but you can easily get to it. You can also open a completely new bank account that they will not have access to and add funds to this account.

Pack and Hide a "Getaway Bag"

While you are busy moving the essentials, make sure you have a separate bag in a separate area that has at least some clothes, cash, and basic necessities such toothpaste, soap, and other necessities for an overnight stay. Make sure that this bag can be grabbed at a moment's notice so that you can just get in the car or in a taxi and leave and know that you will be safe for a few days no matter where you go. The reasoning behind this is that they may become aware of your plans, they may realize where you are planning to go and you will need to change all your plans at a moment's notice.

Gather Evidence of Abuse

Be sure that you can prove abuse. There is a very good chance that your first stop may need to be at the police station to apply for a protection order or even to open a case. When you do this, bring any and all evidence of abuse, such as photographs, voice recordings, videos, previous police reports, and even eyewitnesses. This will make your case stronger and will help with ensuring the authorities take the matter seriously.

Hide an Extra Car Key

If the abuser realizes that you are planning to leave, or if you leave with the abuser present and the situation became violent, the abuser may attempt to take your house and car keys away in an attempt to force you to stay so they can find a way to keep you there long term, whether through mental abuse or physical violence. This is why it's a good idea to have an extra set of keys somewhere you could easily get to them without the abuser being able to intercept you.

Decide Whether You Should Take Your Children With You

If you have children that live with you, you will need to seriously evaluate the risk to them when you leave. You will need to determine the environment that will be the safest for them and what option will be the best for them. Do not stay with the abuser for the sake of the children. If you feel that you cannot take them with you, but that it is a risk to leave them with the abuser, contact a social worker and explain the situation to them. They are trained to handle situations like these.

Step 3: Get Out Fast

When the time comes for you to leave, there should be no hesitation or last-minute preparations. You should be able to act normally and within a blink of an eye, be out of the house, in the car, and out of sight. The abuser should not have time to react or make plans to follow you.

Pick a Safe Time, Not the Right Time

There will never be such a thing as a right time to walk away from the abuser. This is why it is important to pick a safe time. This will be any time the abuser will be out of the house and you will be at home. If you have everything planned correctly, you should be able to leave completely prepared for any scenario in under a minute.

Go Directly to a Safe Place

There is every chance that the abuser might suspect something and could be trying to follow you to see where you go. Or they could return sooner than expected and start looking for you. So when you leave be sure that you go directly to your predetermined safe place that the abuser will not be able to find, lock yourself indoors and wait a while to make sure that they are not waiting for you close by. Also, make sure your phone is switched off, and the battery removed if possible as it is very easy in modern times to track a phone.

Step 4: Once You're Out of the House

So you've made it out of the house, what's next? Well, essentially you will now change your life completely to make it more difficult for the abuser to find you.

Keep Your Whereabouts Secret

Do not tell anyone that may have contact with your abuser where you are. Do not tell co-workers, do not post it on social media, and tell as few people as possible where you are. Keep your whereabouts a secret as long as possible, but at the very least, until the restraining order is in effect.

Change Your Work Habits

If the narcissist cannot find out where you stay, they will start looking for you at other places that they know you will be. This will be your place of work. A blessing of COVID-19 is that employers are more prone to allowing employees to work from home. Speak to your employer as soon as possible and explain the situation to them, find out if you can work from home, transfer to another location even if temporarily or alternatively go on paid time off for as long as possible. In these ways, the abuser will not be able to find you through your work either.

File the Restraining Order

Get a restraining order in place as soon as possible. Especially if your life may be in danger. If the abuser ignores the terms of the restraining order, you can contact the police and take further action against them in court. This will also be valuable evidence if the narcissist does attempt to attack you, and you are forced to protect yourself or someone else has to step in.

Stop All Contact With Your Partner

If you do not break off contact with your partner, they will attempt to manipulate you into returning to them again. If they cannot do this, they will attempt to gather information from you so that they can find you and see where you are hiding.

Don't Leave Clues

When you are preparing your departure and safe house, ensure that there are no clues to what you are planning and where you are going. Make sure that they cannot get hold of your call log history to see where and whom you have called, consider using a burner phone for the planning of your escape. Make sure your phone location is deactivated so they cannot track your location and see where you went. Make sure that if you are purchasing items for this that they are not able to see this on your bank statements or find receipts reflecting this. The same goes for emergency funds.

Make sure they cannot find evidence of this or find the funds. Consider asking friends and co-workers if you can pay money to their account and tell the abuser that you loaned them that money while they give you cash back. You can also sneak small amounts of cashback into your grocery shopping and then get rid of the receipts before the abuser can see them.

Be Prepared to Call 911

The abuser will definitely attempt to find them, and since there is always the possibility that they will become violent, to that end, make sure that you always have a means of contacting emergency assistance. There are also quite a few free applications that can be downloaded on your smartphone that will alert emergency services at the press of a button and even share your location immediately.

Chapter 6:

Step 3—Finding Yourself

Finding Yourself Overview

After we have gotten away from the narcissistic abuse, we need to become reacquainted with ourselves. The narcissist has changed us and changed our perspectives of ourselves. We will have a complete lack of understanding of who we are and what we are capable of. This is why the next step requires us to meet ourselves again and stop seeing ourselves from the perspective of the narcissist.

What Is Self-Discovery?

Self-discovery is a constant journey that we engage in during which time we question and answer every aspect of ourselves. From what our driving force is, to what our dreams and goals are, to what our abilities are, and what our personality traits are. This will eventually culminate into possessing knowledge of ourselves, which will then allow us to make the correct choices in life and head into the correct situations that will allow us to thrive to the top of our abilities.

Importance of Self-Discovery

Discovering and getting to know yourself is quite important. as it allows you to take control back into your own hands and start to live your own life again. This will be your first step toward healing and being independent again. Let's have a look at the benefits of discovering yourself.

Listen to Your Gut

You will have more faith and trust in yourself. This will allow you to listen to your subconscious more, or as it is otherwise known, your gut feelings.

Understand and Know Your Feelings

You will be able to identify your feelings better and understand what caused these feelings in you.

Stand Up for Yourself

Your self-worth will start to increase and it will give you confidence again to stand up for yourself, your opinions, your values, and your own abilities.

Stop Comparing Yourself

You will start seeing the uniqueness and value that you, as an individual, has. This will allow you to stop comparing yourself to others.

Set Boundaries in Relationships

When you start to realize where your boundaries are, what is good for you and what is bad for you, and what you believe, you will be able to more easily set boundaries in relationships. As a result, you will engage in more healthy relationships.

Understand What Holds You Back

You will understand what is holding you back, especially when it comes to major decisions. You will be able to improve on these aspects and help free yourself.

Know What You're Afraid Of

When you understand your fears, you'll be more comfortable facing them. When you are able to face your fears they can no longer be used to control you.

Build Better Habits

You will be able to identify bad habits such as self-isolation and substance dependency. You will be able to identify where they come from and how to turn them around. When you start to turn them around, you will be able to look after yourself and fulfill your needs in all aspects.

Set More Meaningful Goals

You will have a clear idea of what your dreams are in life and what you would like to achieve. When you know what you want, the path to get there will also be more clear so which will allow you to set better and more achievable goals for yourself.

Recognize Your Strengths and Weaknesses

You will start noticing your strengths again, and realize what your actual weaknesses are. This will allow you to use your strength to your own benefit while trying to work on and improve your weaknesses.

Uncover Your Biggest Dreams in Life

Knowing yourself allows you to find out what will make you truly happy in life. This will allow you to discover what your biggest dream in your life is.

Live More Intentionally

When you discover your own beliefs and value system, you will be able to live according to this and will no longer have to go along with the narcissist's idea of what life should be like.

The Self-Discovery Tip

How to Find Yourself After Narcissistic Abuse

Now that we realize the benefits of discovering ourselves, we need to look at how we can go about meeting ourselves again after suffering from narcissistic abuse.

Reflect on How Your Experiences Affected Your Sense of Self

Look back at your entire life, from childhood up until where you currently are. Look at the experiences you have had—how did this make you feel? Look specifically at interactions you've had with other people, especially experiences that had a notable emotional impact on you. How did these experiences and interactions influence what you think about yourself after you had gone through this?

Separate Yourself From the Effects of The Abuse

Look back at the experiences you had and the scars and wounds they left upon you. Specifically, those that changed your perspective. Now, start to imagine that the events did not happen to you. Imagine that this experience did not change you at all. Then find a normal reaction afterward and look at how you would have acted instead. From now on, attempt to imitate that reaction of yours instead of the one you actually had. Accept that you were abused and suffered this trauma, but try not to let it define your actions and emotions.

Get in Touch With Your Real Feelings

The narcissist has most probably reconditioned you to no longer feel your emotions. Instead of feeling them repress them and adopt the reaction of the feeling the narcissist wants you to have. Try how hard we can, however, we cannot fully get rid of our emotions. Start reflecting on your actual emotions and embrace them again.

Reflect on Your Values and Beliefs

Look at the values and beliefs you currently hold, which of them do not feel entirely correct. Which of them falls completely into the realm of what the narcissist believed? Once you have identified these beliefs, ask yourself if you truly believe in these things. If not, what do you actually believe instead?

Focus on What's Good About You

The narcissist will have broken down your self-esteem. They would make you believe that you are incompetent and have no positive traits. Now is the time to reflect on yourself and sort out where they lied to you and where they exaggerated. To better see what your actual good traits are that have been diminished and broken down, look at your past accomplishments and achievements. Look at the praises and awards you have received throughout your life and see if any of these good things you have achieved in your life has been diminished by the narcissist. These are good qualities and abilities about you that you most probably still possess. Focus on these and see if you can regain this and expand on it.

Figure Out What Your Interests, Passions, and Hobbies Are

The narcissist will make you adapt your interests to fall in line with theirs, and they will kill your passion and force you to withdraw from your hobbies. Now you need to explore this again; look at your local community center and see what classes they offer, do any intrigue you or excite you? That is probably what your interests are, and by exploring these, you will once again find hobbies and rekindle your passion.

Think About What You Want Uut of Life

Don't imagine the perfect life or your dream life. Instead, I want you to make a list of realistic wants for your future. Look that things like what career would you like to be in, how much would you like to earn? Where would you like to be living? How would you like to feel, emotionally? What would you like your relationship status to be at that time? The goal of this exercise is to rekindle your interest in your own life and to help you create an achievable idea for your future. A clear direction to work towards.

Accept Who You Are

During this introspection of yourself, you will find some aspects of yourself that are indeed negative. There will be areas and events where you acted poorly and did something wrong. You may feel guilty and bad about this. That is perfectly fine because it means that you realize your mistake and can improve on it. To do this, however, you must accept these mistakes you have made. They are as much a part of you as the good parts are. You need to accept every part of yourself.

Find Ways to Love Yourself

This is probably the most difficult step to take. You have been so conditioned to be disgusted by yourself, to feel that you are worthless, you are inadequate. To now change this mindset is difficult. But this is also a very important step. To start loving yourself, look at where you currently are. You have already had the strength to leave a situation that is bad for you. You have already tried to protect yourself and succeeded. That is a form of sacrifice and self-love and is one of many examples of loveable traits you have.

Do what YOU want to do

Would you like to go to a carnival and eat the biggest coldest ice cream you can find? Do it. Would you like to lounge around naked in your home when you are off? Do it. Some things that you may want to do could be frowned upon by some people that are judgemental. But as long as it is not illegal, you should sometimes just go crazy and do something that you want to for absolutely no reason. This is a way of allowing yourself to explore your inner child, your own enjoyment, and your own happiness. This is needed to really get to know yourself.

Helpful Self-Discovery Techniques

We've looked at some steps we can take in the previous section. In this section, I would like to just look at some extra tips and techniques that you could use.

Start a Morning Journaling Practice

In the morning when you wake up, start your day with a journal entry. Write down the dreams you had during the night. How did they make you feel? What do you think your dreams meant? Can you see the connection between your dreams and the events of the previous day? What are some of the events from the previous day that stood out and affected you? What is your wish for the day waiting for you? What do you not want in the day awaiting you? These are a few thoughts you can focus on and write down that help you to have a bit of a look into your subconscious mind and how it processes your everyday life.

Make a List of Things That Delight You

Make a list of things that make you feel more comfortable in your life and a list of things that make you less comfortable. Try to start engaging more in your lists of comfortable things and stop engaging with the things on your uncomfortable list.

Consider Meditation or Yoga

Practices like meditation or yoga are based on spiritual beliefs, but you do not need to share the beliefs to make use of these practices. These are two practices that are used to calm your mind and gain introspective on yourself. You can attempt to start one of these as a hobby to help you focus your mind.

Consider Leaving Your Comfort Zone

One of the best ways to learn more about yourself is by moving outside your comfort zone. This is not saying that you should do things that will make you uncomfortable. Rather, look for activities and events that you are not sure you would enjoy or not, and then take a chance on them.

Use Self-Affirmations

Self-affirmations are little mantra's that you can tell yourself to help you build up your own confidence and even energize yourself. These will be quotes and sentences like "This will be the best day of my life that I've had so far."

Don't Hide Your Imperfections

Instead of mimicking the narcissist by also trying to put up a mask that makes you seem perfect, show the world that you are better than them because you can accept your imperfections. When someone sees that you have the confidence to be yourself and that you are not trying to deceive them, they will have more respect for you and your boundaries. This will allow you to be more comfortable, promote responsibility, and allow you to feel more comfortable.

Find Who You Are Not

Look at the influences throughout your entire life and see what influences have left you with views that you do not agree with. Explore and see where these influences came from and explore the difference between you and the influence, do not disregard the impact it had on you, but focus on the difference and you'll soon realize that by seeing what you are not, you will see what you actually are.

Focus on What is Right With You

The old saying goes, "There is no harsher critic than you yourself." and this is quite true. We tend to consistently think of ourselves in a negative light, and never in a good light. These negative thoughts are even more prominent after narcissistic abuse. The trick I want to explain here is that every time your inner critic tries to say something negative, you reply to it with a list of about three positive things about yourself. Drown the negative with the positive.

Find Solace in Solitude

Sometimes we need to just be alone. This can, however, be scary after we had gone through narcissistic abuse, especially because we no longer know ourselves and may feel like strangers to ourselves. This is however the best way to get to know a stranger, to be alone with them for a period of time.

Act Authentically

This last one is also especially difficult for survivors of abuse. You have become so used to acting in a way that will make others happy, or in a way that others expect you to act. If you were to be authentic to yourself, you will base your actions not on how you think others want you to act, but instead on what will make you comfortable and give you enjoyment.

Self-Discovery Questions

These will be questions that you can ask yourself in order to help you on your self-discovery journey. The honest answers to these questions will help you to get to know yourself.

The Self

These are questions that relate to your personality and your interests in life.

- What is the purpose of my life?

- What type of personality do I possess?

- Am I allocating a healthy amount of time to my social life?

- What inspires me?

- What brings me joy?

- What is the most important to me at the moment?

- What's something that I would like to direct my energy toward and why?

- In which ways have I been holding myself back?

- What is keeping me from being happy?

- How can I increase my happiness?

Values

These questions will focus on your values and belief system.

- What are the five most important values for you in regard to your personal values?

- What are the five most important values for you in regard to your professional values?

- How are you compromising on your values in your life?

- How do you feel responsible to influence the world with your values?

- How are you compromising your integrity?

Courage and Fear

These questions will look at what scares you and what makes you confident.

- What is your single largest fear?

- Have any of your fears ever been realized?

- Would you be able to overcome your fears if you test yourself on them?

- Which of your current choices could require you to have more confidence?

Experiences

These questions will focus on your experiences in your life.

- What lessons have you learned from your most recent experiences?

- What experiences in your life allow you to go on living?

- What is one experience you have always wanted to embark on

Chapter 7:

Step 4—Practicing Self-Compassion

Self-Compassion Overview

What Is Self-Compassion?

Think of the compassion that you feel towards others. Compassion has three steps. First, you notice that somebody is suffering in some way. Secondly, you feel moved by their pain. Lastly, you realize that all humans share this pain in some way or form and that it is human to feel this. Now apply that same thinking to yourself. You must acknowledge that you are suffering from pain, then you must allow yourself to feel this pain, and you must accept that this pain makes you human.

Importance of Self-Compassion After Experiencing Narcissistic Abuse

Self-compassion will allow you to accept and embrace every part of you, it will allow you to share empathy with yourself. You will be able to accept and understand your past actions. By doing so, you will be able to enjoy yourself even more now, and not feel weighed down by your own past actions. This will also help you to undo some of the damage from the narcissist as they have been using your normal human mistakes to break you down.

A few more benefits of feeling compassion for yourself will include:

- Your overall health will improve.

- You will feel value in yourself again.

- You will be less likely to suffer from emotional outbursts.

- You will feel more pleased with your life as it currently is.

- You will find it easier to make and maintain social connections.

- Negative emotions will be diminished.

- You will feel more comfortable admitting your mistakes and attempting to correct them

- You will feel more comfortable in your own body.

The Three Essential Elements of Self-Compassion

As I said at the start of this chapter, compassion consists of three steps. These three steps can also be closely compared to the three core elements of self-compassion, which we will have a closer look at now.

Mindfulness

Mindfulness is the act of observing our pain and trauma with a disconnected state of mind. We do not become overwhelmed by our emotions and we do not become obsessed with them. At this moment, we simply observe them and acknowledge that they are there. In this way, we can face the reality of the moment, we can actively observe our entire reaction to this situation, and we can realize our thoughts and assess them with clarity. It allows us a form of introspection and acceptance of a situation without any further trauma or emotional impact.

Self-Kindness

This allows us to feel supportive of ourselves. We feel compassion for ourselves and this allows us to comfort and encourage ourselves whether we are suffering from pain inflicted on us from an outside source or from inside ourselves. Instead of judging ourselves for our shortcomings, we show kindness to ourselves.

Common Humanity

This is perhaps the most important element of self-compassion. Common humanity teaches us that all humans are inherently flawed. This is what makes us human, in fact. Failing teaches us how to succeed, hardship makes us stronger, and pain waits for each of us.

Details of Self-Compassion

Now that we understand self-compassion, we need to understand how we can enact this in our daily lives.

What Self-Compassion Is Not

We can learn a lot about how to enact Self-Compassion in our lives by looking at the misconceptions of self-compassion.

Self-Compassion Is Not Self-Pity

We are not feeling pity for ourselves when we show self-compassion. In fact, it is quite the opposite. We do not feel sorry for ourselves and we do not feel depressed over this. We only accept that we have done something wrong and that we have the capability to make mistakes.

Self-Compassion Is Not Self-Indulgence

The difference between self-compassion and self-indulgence is that during self-indulgence we will often misuse the concept of compassion to allow ourselves to over-indulge ourselves. Like saying I accidentally embarrassed myself, therefore I'll drink myself into a blackout drunk state tonight.

Self-Compassion Is Not Self-Esteem

Self-esteem can be quite problematic. Too low self-esteem can cause depression and a poor sense of worth, whereas too high self-esteem can cause other problems such as narcissism. The main difference here is that self-esteem is based on a value that is decided by what you believe you are worth based on your actions and what you can achieve. Where self-compassion does not care about any perceived value.

Self-Compassion Is Not a Weakness

Many people believe that being compassionate towards themselves and accepting that they not only have flaws but emotional flaws as well, proves that they are weak and being controlled by their emotions. This is, in fact, quite the opposite. When we are too scared to admit that we have emotions, we are in fact being controlled by fear and guilt. As soon as you feel compassionate to yourself regarding these feelings, you can overcome them.

Self-Compassion Is Not Complacence

There is a belief that if you feel compassion towards yourself instead of critiquing your own shortcomings, you will lose motivation. The belief is that you will consistently say, "It's okay that I made a mistake, I'm just human." Instead of, "I should not be making mistakes, I need to try and be better." This is, in fact, not true. The compassion narrative is more along the lines of, "It's human to make mistakes, and I am only human after all. I can always try better next time but do not need to dwell on mistakes of the past."

Self-Compassion Is Not Narcissism

Being able to accept and move on from your shortcomings and mistakes often appears to those looking in from the outside as if you believe that you do not have these shortcomings. When someone looks in from the outside, they do not always see the turmoil that exists within us and how we work through our own trauma. This lack of perspective is what causes the misconception that being able to accept your mistakes is equal to completely denying the existence of these shortcomings.

Self-Compassion Is Not Selfishness

In a society that still largely believes that "We do anything for family." When we then take time away from our schedule and other people in our lives to care for ourselves it seems as if we do not care about their well-being and place our own desires above theirs. Although a bit of selfishness is completely healthy, taking a small amount of time to ensure that you are emotionally and mentally healthy enough to ensure you have the capacity to still look after others is the exact opposite of being selfish.

How to Practice Self-Compassion

Now that we have a clearer understanding of self-compassion and what it is, we can look into how we can practice this to help ourselves. Below are some techniques for practicing self-compassion that you could use.

Recognize That You're Human

You need to understand that you are simply human. Your abilities are limited by what humans can do. The reason why we tend to set goals for ourselves that are unobtainable by normal standards is because a narcissist has already conditioned us to believe that anything less than superhuman is not good enough. When we realize that we are only human and set goals that are attainable by human standards, we will finally be able to achieve our goals again, and in doing so improve the way in which we see ourselves.

Be Mindful of Negative Self-Focused Thoughts

Have you ever entered or exited a room during a power outage and found yourself attempting to switch on the light? This is because we are creatures of habit. Even when we know our habits will not achieve the usual goal, we will still absent-mindedly follow these habits. Our thoughts do the same thing. When we are in the habit of thinking negatively about ourselves, we will continue to do so without realizing it. We need to start realizing that just because we have a negative thought about ourselves once in a while, does not mean these thoughts are true. If we use mindfulness when we come across these thoughts, we will be able to effectively process these thoughts without allowing them to break us down any further.

Practice Self-Care

Take some time once in a while to look after yourself. Practice some of the self-care techniques that we will explore in the next chapter. The idea behind self-care is that you act in a way completely opposite to your negative thoughts and low self-esteem habitats.

Validate Your Emotions

We often try to reject certain emotions that we feel. These are usually the emotions that the narcissist did not approve of. When we reject our emotions, we increase our own emotional distress. The reason for this is that we experience emotions for a reason and rejecting them goes against our nature. When we validate our emotions, accept them and allow ourselves to feel them, we will be able to listen to these emotions.

Reduce Self-Destructive Behaviors

When we lack self-compassion, we will engage in self-destructive behavior. This is often our way of coping as well as punishing ourselves for behavior we do not find acceptable. This usually presents itself as eating disorders, self-harm, or substance abuse. When we look into impulse control techniques and break away from these self-destructive behaviors, we are already practicing a method of self-compassion.

Practice Acts of Kindness

We often measure our own value by what we can do for others. Although defending this is not healthy, there is a way we can healthily do this, however. If you realize that you cannot find a way to help yourself, the best way may be to engage in activities such as volunteering at a homeless shelter or soup kitchen. This could give you a feeling of accomplishment and value.

Recognize Your Accomplishments

Look into other situations you have been a part of and experiences you have gone through. These are accomplishments that you have already achieved. You have most definitely been through a difficult time in your life and the fact that you survived it and came through this situation means that you have accomplished something already. Remember these situations and what you did to successfully get through this.

Third Person Self-Talk (Self-Distancing)

If you find yourself in a stressful situation or in a period of distress, change your way of thinking about yourself. Instead of thinking of yourself in the first-person start thinking of yourself in the third person as if you are referring to another person. You are usually harsher on yourself than on other people, and if you can think of yourself as another person, you will cut yourself some slack.

Learn the Basics of Cluster B Personality Disorders

A narcissist is a very good example of someone with cluster B personality disorder. These are people that usually succeed in life at the expense of others. They are the type of people that will abuse, manipulate and exploit others. If you learn more about these types of personality disorders, you could better understand the trauma they have put you through.

Tap Into Your Desire for Self-Preservation and Safety

Part of the abuse from a narcissist breaks down your natural sense of self-preservation. They do this to get you to better put their needs before your own, and so you allow them to continuously abuse you. You will need to regain this desire to remain safe and preserve your own life. This will allow you to regain control over your life and is another achievement you can boast about.

Strive to Shift Direction

It is often difficult for us to accept that our partner, the person that we have fallen in love with and adore so much, is actually an abusive person. It can be even more difficult to accept that this partner of ours may have a disorder that led them to do these horrible things to us. But we do need to accept the harsh truth. We need to be able to prepare ourselves mentally and even physically to accept the truth of the matter so that we can stop blaming ourselves and start reversing the damage they have done to us.

Avoid Toxic People and Situations

If you leave one abusive and toxic environment, but either enter another or remain in another, you will not heal and continue to be abused. This will almost be like substituting an alcohol addiction for a drug addiction. Be sure that you constantly take a hard look at the situations and environments you find yourself in so you do not get pulled into another situation like the one you are attempting to heal from.

Avoid Behaviors That Can Increase the Bond to the Abuser

Ideally, you should be going no contact with your abuser. This is not always possible; however, if you had kids together or were married. Even if you find yourself in a situation like this with your abuser, you should try to avoid anything that can either strengthen or reawaken the bond that you had with them. This will be behavior such as reading old texts from them or looking at old pictures, going to places where you had good memories with them, like the restaurant where you had your first date. Doing these actions will make you miss them more and allow them to lure you back into their trap.

Actively Work to Banish Negative Self-Talk

Have a constant eye on what you are saying and how you say it, especially when it is about you. If you find yourself mid-sentence of breaking yourself down or insulting yourself, try to change the rest of the sentence into something positive. Imagine you are talking to your child when you are talking about yourself. Would you break them down or built them up?

Maintain Patience With Yourself

Don't feel like you should be completely fine the moment you walk out of the relationship, or even try to compare this to other relationships. This is a completely different type of pain and trauma that you are experiencing. The narcissist created a type of abuse unique to you, which means the recovery will be unique as well and it may take longer than what you are used to, to heal from this.

Self-Compassion Affirmations

Using affirmations are amazing ways to practice self-compassion. They help you to say something positive to yourself, and could even help you notice some parts of yourself that still need to be accepted. I've gathered a list of affirmations for you here. I would advise you to write them down and place them in random places for you to find; set a reminder on your phone every day at a random time with an affirmation as the title. Do what you can to incorporate these affirmations into your daily life so you have at least one of these affirmations brighten up your day.

- I deserve kindness, especially from myself.

- I am allowed to make mistakes, and I am allowed to forgive myself.

- I am prioritizing myself today.

- The good and the bad are both parts of me.

- I am not perfect, I am unique.

- I can be compassionate towards myself.

- Every mistake I make is another lesson I get to learn.

- Every day is an opportunity to learn.

- Emotions are normal, it's my body's way of talking to me, and I can listen to it.

- When I make a mistake, I remind myself that I am alive.

- Sadness is a part of the human cycle, and I am allowed to gently console myself.

- As long as I've tried, I have already succeeded.

Chapter 8:

Step 5—All About Self-Care

Self-Care Overview

What Is Self-Care?

This is a way to look after ourselves, to make sure that our needs are met, and that we are healthy. When we ensure that we are taken care of, we can better take care of those around us that need us. For me, self-care is the healthiest of boundaries. It is literally a collection of activities or hobbies that make us feel refreshed and ready for the day. The best thing is that everyone's self-care is unique to themselves and nobody can tell you that you are doing it wrong or that you should be doing it their way.

Why Is Self-Care Important?

Self-care helps you to refocus yourself, set safe boundaries as well as allows you to replenish energy. Let's look at some of the benefits that self-care can give us.

Self-Care Improves Resilience

When you have a proper self-care plan and you actually look after yourself and the negative effects of stress are greatly diminished. This is because you actually manage to relieve some of the stress and tension on you. When you have accomplished this, your reactions and responses to life will be easier to control and decide.

Self-Care Increases Feelings of Worthiness

We are always looking out for everyone else. We have deadlines at work, friends that need help, partners to look after, and just so much to do that we feel are important. Through this sea of important factors, we tend to overlook ourselves. When we make sure that we spend a healthy amount of time taking care of ourselves, we realize how important we actually are as well. This will help us to feel that we are actually worthy of everything and everyone around us.

Self-Care Improves Feelings of Well-Being

When we allow our mind, our emotions, and our body to heal, and release the tension and stress, we soon realize that this makes us feel better overall. Our mind no longer feels cloudy, our emotions no longer feel overwhelming, and our body no longer feels tired all the time.

Self-Care Benefits Everyone Around You

With all this energy and good feelings inside of you, you cannot help but transfer them to those around you. When someone speaks to you and requires your attention, it no longer feels like a chore. You may find yourself more interested and more engaging, even friendlier. This can help to build up people around you, and promote healthier relationships with them.

Self-Care Increases Self-Confidence

When you feel worthy, friendly, well rested, and just completely revitalized your confidence will increase naturally, and the great thing about this is when you feel more confident you will feel even better and more worthy, you will start having this cycle of positivity that can help you get through an entire day with an actual smile!

Self-Care Reduces Stress and Anxiety

The resilience self-care gives you means that you can handle stress and anxiety better, but at the same time, self-care helps you to have lower levels of stress and anxiety. When you care for yourself, the tension will just melt out of your body.

Self-Care Improves Sleep Quality and Digestion

When your mind and body are calmer, more at ease and less anxious, it actually allows you to enter a state of sleep a lot faster. This is because your body will relax faster, and your mind will not be as busy assessing, reassessing, planning, worrying, and thinking the entire time. This will also mean that your body is no longer in a constant state of high alert, which will allow your digestive system to speed up again. You see, when the body is tensed and ready for something to go wrong, it slows down the digestive system so that it can store more energy for longer, just in case you need it to survive.

Self-Care Improves Focus

Now that you are no longer allocating your focus and energy to all the stress, insecurities, and just plain fatigue, your mind has enough energy to focus on what you want it to. So when you need to focus on something, there are fewer things for your mind to wander to, and it can even maintain the focus for longer!

Self-Care Boosts Your Immune System

When your stress levels are lower, and your digestive system is faster, it actually influences your immune system as well. It suddenly becomes stronger and more confident, just like you! This also means less time feeling all sickish and groggy, so even more time for you to care for yourself!

Self-Care Increases Productivity

With all the extra energy and focus that you have, you will be able to accomplish your tasks faster and with more ease. This will make your productivity levels skyrocket! And we know what that means, another part of this positivity cycle as you will feel more fulfilled, more confident in your abilities, and more worthy of your place in life.

Types of Self-Care

Now that we understand the value of self-care and what it can offer us, let's look at the different types of self-care available to us.

Physical Self-Care

The wonderful thing about self-care is that when I say we're going to start at the basics, I really do mean the basics. Physical self-care can be simple things such as brushing your teeth, having a shower or bath, getting enough sleep, and having something to eat. Now yes, this may sound like things we usually do every day, but when we are feeling down and depressed, it is often hard to just get out of bed, and then the basics start to feel like impossible tasks.

Emotional Self-Care

Emotional self-care is made up of the things you do to make you laugh, feel content, or be full of anticipation. To achieve emotional self-care can be as easy as switching off the news for a few hours, reading a book, or even watching a comedy. Anything that provokes a positive emotional state that you enjoy.

Social Self-Care

Social self-care will depend very much on your personality, whether you are an introvert or extrovert, and how much you actually enjoy social interactions. For one person, social self-care could be taking a step back from social interactions, as they could already be feeling overwhelmed from a busy day at work where they had to see a lot of people. Where others could see social self-care as going out to a bar or restaurant where there are a lot of people and they can fulfill their social requirements as they may enjoy this. This is why your self-care routine is so personal.

Spiritual Self-Care

You do not actually have to be very religious or spiritual to practice spiritual self-care. You may have noticed that I didn't mention exercise during the physical self-care section, that is because it fits in so much nicer here. Exercise can be akin to meditation and yoga, or even just being out in nature. That is because these are usually times when you gain the most immersion into your own values and beliefs, and this is what spiritual self-care is all about.

Personal Self-Care

This is where you take the time to get to know the true you and look after this person. Personal self-care will focus more on things such as your hobbies or pushing your boundaries by trying something brand new, even if it's just a food item you have never tried.

Environmental Self-Care

This is usually your immediate surroundings, like your office space and your home. Don't worry, I'm not going to suggest you do regular spring cleaning unless that is something that you enjoy. Instead, this can be something as simple as putting a comfortable blanket on your couch that you can cuddle up under, or placing a few pictures of your loved ones in areas where you spend a lot of time, like in your car. This helps you to feel more comfortable and relaxed in these environments.

Financial Self-Care

This could be a tricky part of self-care, especially in our modern economy. The good news however is that financial self-care is not just about saving money and drawing up budgets, it could be something as simple as listening to a podcast on finances or seeing if there are any old and unused items in your house that you may be able to sell for a bit of money, even if you don't need that money at the moment.

Professional Self-Care

We need a proper balance between our actual life, and our career lives. You need to be able to switch off and take a breath so that you can recover and gear up for the next workday. This however does not mean you need to set hard boundaries. If you are someone that enjoys their work and can put in extra hours without it becoming detrimental to your life and mental health then it is perfectly fine. There are also smaller boundaries you can set in place such as refusing to eat in the office at lunchtime.

Intellectual Self-Care

Intellectual self-care is about keeping your mind healthy and is a great way to help you with finding interesting topics of conversation for future use. This will also help you feel that you are making progress and bettering yourself which can lead to a variety of benefits. It can be as easy as going onto Wikipedia or just listening to a podcast.

How to Practice Self-Care

How To

Assess Your Needs

To be able to properly care for ourselves, we need to make sure that we know our needs. Make a list of all the aspects of a normal day for yourself and what the major activities of a normal day are for you.

Consider Your Stressors

Look at the cause of your stress and see if you can think of any way to reduce the impact these factors have on you.

Devise Self-Care Strategies

Plan out your self-care routine and activities. See how you can implement them in your daily life and address your stress influences.

Plan for Challenges

Life is full of twists and turns. When you start to focus on one aspect of your life then other aspects may suffer from this. Be sure that you are prepared to notice this and address these arising challenges.

Take Small Steps

Don't worry about addressing all your stress influences at once. Start out small and don't worry about getting everything done immediately. If you can make one small improvement every day, you'll make major changes in your life without being overwhelmed.

Schedule Time to Focus on Your Needs

If we don't set out a specific time every day to look after ourselves, we tend to completely forget about ourselves. This is exactly why we need to make sure that we schedule our self-care. This way no matter what goes wrong or how busy we get, we can be sure that we'll be able to look after ourselves.

Build a Healthy Foundation

Build yourself a steady routine that will help you to ensure you have a good foundation to start your self–care routine. It could be something like ensuring you have a decent sleep routine, make sure you eat at least something healthy once per day, and that you start every day by doing something positive to yourself, like working on your hobby, having a shower as soon as you wake up, or just having some sort of mental input.

Avoid Stress

Look at what causes you stress and try to avoid these influences. Take enough breaks from work, social media, and other high-stress environments. Most importantly, learn to say no to what causes you stress or discomfort.

Relax

Make sure that you have ways to relax, and times when your mind and body can shut down and refresh. This can be achieved by doing simple activities like just reading a book, playing a board game with family or friends, or playing music that relaxes you while you are doing other activities. These are just a few ideas, but the possibilities of relaxation are endless.

Get Outside

Fresh air and a bit of nature can be amazing to our mental and physical health. Look into taking a daily walk, or going for a hike at least once per month. Make plans for a picnic in the park, or on the beach. Any way to allow you outside for a few hours per week. Even if it's just sitting in your garden for a while.

Get Social

Be sure to give yourself social input as well. Do not become isolated, but do not overwhelm yourself. This could be something as simple as having a video call with a friend, going out to a movie, or just engaging with an online community where you have an actual conversation instead of just making and replying to a few comments.

Chapter 9:

Step 6—Be Patient and Let

Time Do Its Work

The Patience Overview

What Is Patience?

When we talk about patience, most people think that we are just talking about being able to wait longer before we become angry at something or someone. This is not the entirety of patience, however. Think of a chain-smoker sitting through dinner at a fancy restaurant without going outside for their fix. They'll probably be a bit irritated by the end of the dinner, and will be craving a cigarette after an hour or two. But when they wait until after dinner to have a cigarette, they are also displaying patience.

Benefits of Cultivating Patience

Helps Focus on Long-Term Goals

You will be more prepared to wait to achieve your goals over a long period of time. When you are impatient, you will want to see results immediately and may engage in activities or ideas that you think may be able to help us achieve this faster. Often these schemes are more detrimental to our goals than it is productive. With patience, we will be more comfortable waiting to achieve our goals and working on smaller seemingly tedious tasks first.

Make More Rational Choices

When we are patient, our emotions are less likely to take over. When someone is frustrating us but we are patient enough, we could find a way to either remove ourselves from the conversation without any conflict. At the same time, we could be calmer after being involved in an accident. These are just some examples of rational choices we may be able to make when we have the patience to control our emotions.

Builds Our Reputation for Persistence

Patience could also allow you to hold out longer when you don't want to be in a certain situation.

Helps to Develop a Skill Set

Learning a new skill is extremely difficult. Patience helps us to endure this. We are willing to remain a bit frustrated longer in order to get to our results. Think of learning a new language; there are so many nuances in speech patterns and when to use certain words and when not to use some adjectives. Every language has its own rules, and learning them will definitely take time and lots of patience.

Makes You a People Magnet

In any and every social relationship, there will be some strain once in a while. We will accidentally offend our friends at least a couple of dozen times. The question is who you would rather spend time with, the friend that has the patience to accept it and work through their emotions, or the person that will immediately blow their top? This is why patience will attract people to you.

Better Mental Health

Impatience promotes stress. When you are more patient, these stress factors will be diminished, instead of running after the next goal, achievement, or experience you refuse to wait for, you will now be waiting for it and letting it happen, which means those feelings of having to always be on the run and be busy will be less. This will improve your mental health quite a lot.

Better Physical Health

When your mental health has improved, your body reacts to it. When your body reacts to this, it will feel better itself, giving you more energy. You will also have more patience to stick with a training plan or other forms of physical improvement.

Makes You Feel Good

With all the extra energy, the feeling of self-worth, and kindness around you when you are patient, you will start to feel better in general. Patience also means that negative influencers have a lesser impact on you. All these aspects of patience will make you feel happier and more content with life.

It Can Bring You Peace

When you are impatient and in a stressful situation, you start to feel discouraged because it seems like it's just not passing. However when you are patient these feelings go away, and even in stressful situations, you will feel more at peace with life and your decisions.

Patience

What Patience Is and Isn't

We understand patience and what it can give us, but I would like to still have a closer look at exactly what patience both is and isn't. This can help us to understand when we make innocent mistakes while trying to practice patience.

Patience Is

We need to look into the aspects of what true patience includes. When you are trying to be patient, look at these traits of yourself and try to focus on improving them. When you get into the habit of practicing these traits to improve your patience, you will eventually find that it happens naturally.

These are the aspects of patience to focus on:

- calm

- persevering

- tolerant

- understanding

- compassionate

- mindful

- hopeful

Patience Isn't

When we try to practice patience, there are certain aspects of our personality we need to try to avoid. These are the personality traits that cause us to be less patient and have a negative impact on our lives.

Try to avoid these personality traits:

- impulsive

- complaining

- judgmental

- pessimistic

- hasty

- granitic

- anxious

Types of Patience

When we think of patience, we normally just think of not having a short temper or being able to wait for something to be delivered that we are excited about.

This is not the only type of patience though. So let's explore the different types of patience.

Interpersonal Patience

This is the type of patience we normally think of. The patience towards other people. Whether we think they are acting too slowly or we think they have bad behavior. If we work on interpersonal patience, we are able to better tolerate the influences of other people in our lives.

Life Hardship Patience

This is when we are waiting for a change in our life. Whether we are currently going through a bad time in our life, or are working on getting a promotion at work. If we can improve our life hardship and patience, we may be able to accept our environment more.

Daily Hassles Patience

These are the aspects that are completely out of our control that we have to deal with. This will be things like being stuck in traffic or waiting for a video to buffer. When you work on this, you will be able to accept that life takes its time.

How to Become Patient

Identify When You're Impatient and What Emotion You're Feeling

When you start to feel impatient, look at the emotions that arise inside of you. What is making you feel this way? Is it anger, anxiety, sadness, or excitement? Then look at what the reason behind this emotion is.

Reframe How You Think About the Situation

Change your thoughts on the situation. Instead of thinking that this is happening to you, think about how this is affecting others as well. Look at the cause of the situation and realize that it is not directed at you and most probably not done on purpose.

Think With Your Purpose in Mind

Keep your sights on your purpose. It's okay if you are delayed in reaching that goal that you have set. You are still making progress getting towards it even if something went wrong.

Learn to Be a Good Listener

When we are in a conversation that we may not specifically be interested in or with someone we might not like, we tend to get impatient. However, if we learn how to become better listeners, it will help us in situations like these to not become bored and impatient.

Accept What You Can't Change

One of the many triggers of impatience is when we say, "I wish I could just change this." When the ice cream machine is broken at your favorite fast food place, or there is some parade going through town on the street of your preferred coffee shop, you cannot change this. We need to learn how to accept the unchangeable aspects of life to achieve patience.

Understand the Symptoms of Feeling Impatient

Sometimes we do not even realize we are impatient. We just think we are being irritable for no reason. The truth is that you most probably are being impatient, and your body can tell you this. We have certain ways that we react to our feelings and when we learn how our body reacts, we can not only identify when we are impatient, but we can counteract this feeling.

Take a Break

This is not just stopping what you are doing and breathing for a moment. The idea is to take a break from your normal day, but specifically from whatever is a repeat offender of making you feel impatient.

Seek Out Support

Sometimes just talking to someone is all we need to feel better. We can feel even better if that person helps us to find a way to improve our reactions and mindset. When you feel overwhelmed by your impatience, find a trusted person you can speak to. Make sure this conversation will, however, be productive and not just complaining, as this could make you feel even worse.

Take Up a Patience-Centric Sport

What better way to learn how to be patient than to practice it and then get rewarded for it? Sports like golf and baseball require a lot of patience from us and can be great teachers to this point.

Recognize the Communal Benefits of Patience

When you become more patient, you have more time for others. You do not get tired of hearing about their problems as fast as you normally do, and you start to realize that you are not just hearing about their problems. They trust and respect you, and when you are patient enough to share your kindness, you benefit all those around you.

Learn to Be Comfortable With Cognitive Dissonance

We've touched on what cognitive dissonance is already, but there are much more mundane ways that we can experience cognitive dissonance that we may not always realize.

Don't Take Life Too Seriously

One reason we tend to become impatient is that we plan out our life and day, sometimes down to the second, without realizing it. Once in a while, it's necessary to just let it all go, accept that you will be late, accept that the water pipe is going to burst at the worst possible time, and then even look for reasons to laugh about it!

Know When Patience Isn't Helpful

If someone wrongs you deliberately, it's a good thing to remain patient and calm with them and sort everything out in a decent manner, but if they continuously wrong you while you remain calm and unphased, they will start to take advantage of this fact. Know where to draw the line.

Conclusion

So, we've learned. We know exactly what a narcissist is. How they manipulate and use you so they can feed off the power they have over us. We've seen how to spot them; when that charming person walks up to us and starts to love-bomb us, we know to be careful of them.

For those of us who are currently in a relationship with a narcissist, you now have the tools to get out, heal, and recover from the damage that they have done to you, but you have more than that. You have my faith in you. If you ever wonder if someone believes in you and roots for you, you have at least one person here. My wish for you is to get out safely and rebuild yourself and your life using these 6 steps I've shared with you.

If you ever feel discouraged throughout your recovery journey, just remember the success story we looked at early on in the book. It is definitely possible to get away from the narcissist for good.

I hope that I now conclude this book with a very different reader than the one that started this book. I am sure that in these pages you have found a completely different person, the real you. Let this person be happy, safe, and free.

I wish you good luck with your new life, free from the narcissist. And I hope that you never have to read this book again.

References

Abuse Warrior. (2021, March 20). *41 Manipulation Tactics Used By Narcissists, Psychopaths, And Sociopaths.* Abuse Warrior. https://abusewarrior.com/abuse/manipulation-tactics/

Aimlief. (2021, January 4). *19 Top Reasons Why Self Discovery Is Important.* Aimlief. https://aimlief.com/why-is-self-discovery-so-important/

Arabi, S. (2017, August 21). *11 Signs Youre the Victim of Narcissistic Abuse.* Psych Central. https://psychcentral.com/blog/recovering-narcissist/2017/08/11-signs-youre-the-victim-of-narcissistic-abuse#1

Arluck, K. (2018, September 12). *Why Do People Fall in Love With Narcissists?* Psychology Today. Www.psychologytoday.com. https://www.psychologytoday.com/us/blog/ask-the-therapist/201809/why-do-people-fall-in-love-narcissists

Atkinson, A. (n.d.). *The Secret to Finding Yourself After a Toxic Relationship* QueenBeeing. Retrieved September 9, 2022, from https://queenbeeing.com/ithe-secret-to-finding-yourself/

Bahadur, N. (2018, November 8). *9 Facts to Know About Narcissistic Personality Disorder Before Calling Someone a Narcissist.* SELF. https://www.self.com/story/narcissistic-personality-disorder-facts

Belle, K. (2016, September 29). *The 7 Startling Stages Of Falling In Love With A Narcissist.* YourTango. https://www.yourtango.com/2016294567/seven-vicious-stages-falling-love-with-narcissist

BetterHelp Editorial Team. (2022, July 7). *The Importance of Setting Boundaries: 10 Benefits for You and Your Relationships* BetterHelp. https://www.betterhelp.com/advice/general/the-importance-of-setting-boundaries-10-benefits-for-you-and-your-relationships/

Browne, S. (2021, January 12). *10 Self-Exploration Practices to Discover Your True Self.* Lifehack. https://www.lifehack.org/896213/self-exploration

Buck, M. (2016, August 2). *32 Self-compassion Affirmations* FaithLoveJourney. https://faithlovejourney.com/affirmations/32-self-compassion-affirmations/

C, P. (2021, November 11). *6 Reasons You Attract Narcissists Into Your Life* Psych2Go. https://psych2go.net/6-reasons-you-attract-narcissists-into-your-life/

Cherry, K. (2018). *How Important Is the Hippocampus in the Brain?* Verywell Mind.

https://www.verywellmind.com/what-is-the-hippocampus-2795231

Cuncic, A. (2021, November 18). *Effects of Narcissistic Abuse.* Verywell Mind. https://www.verywellmind.com/effects-of-narcissistic-abuse-5208164#:~:text=Narcissistic%20abuse%20is%20a%20type

Davenport, B. (2020, August 20). *11 Damaging After Effects Of Emotional Abuse.* Live Bold and Bloom. https://liveboldandbloom.com/08/emotional-abuse/after-effects-emotional-abuse

Destiny's Odyssey. (n.d.). *Self-Discovery - Self Awareness - our inner self.* Destinysodyssey.com. Retrieved September 9, 2022, from https://destinysodyssey.com/personal-development/self-discovery/

DiGiulio, S. (2019, July 9). *How to train yourself to be more patient.* NBC News. https://www.nbcnews.com/better/lifestyle/how-train-yourself-be-more-patient-ncna1022356

Dimaggio, G. (2020, July 9). *10 Things to Know About Narcissistic Personality Disorder.* Psychiatric Times. https://www.psychiatrictimes.com/view/10-things-know-about-narcissistic-personality-disorder?page=3

Earnshaw, E. (2019, July 20). *6 Types of boundaries you deserve to have (and how to maintain them).* MindBodyGreen.

https://www.mindbodygreen.com/articles/six-types-of-boundaries-and-what-healthy-boundaries-look-like-for-each

Estee @ Hopeful Panda. (2021, October 22). *How to Find Yourself After Narcissistic Abuse.* Hopeful Panda. https://hopefulpanda.com/how-to-find-yourself-after-narcissistic-abuse/

Fraser, R. (2021, October 14). *Narcissistic abuse survivor shares her inspiring story. Stylist.* https://www.stylist.co.uk/relationships/narcissistic-abuse-toxic-relationship/547141

Freeman, R. (2015, January 25). *Nine Steps Toward Self Compassion After an Abusive Relationship. Neuroinstincts* Dr. Rhonda Freeman. https://neuroinstincts.com/nine-steps-toward-the-road-to-self-compassion-after-an-abusive-relationship/

Fritscher, L. (2019). *Depersonalization/Derealization Disorder Causes Feelings of Detachment.* Verywell Mind. https://www.verywellmind.com/derealization-2671582

Good Therapy. (n.d.). Patience. GoodTherapy.org Therapy Blog. Retrieved September 10, 2022, from https://www.goodtherapy.org/blog/psychpedia/patience

Gupta, S. (2022, August 15). *What Is the Narcissistic Abuse Cycle?* Verywell Mind.

https://www.verywellmind.com/narcissistic-abuse-cycle-stages-impact-and-coping-6363187#:~:text=The%20narcissistic%20abuse%20cycle%20refers

Hankins, M. (2020, October 26). *The Three Types of Patience - How To Be More Patient*. HumblHuman. https://humblhuman.com/the-three-types-of-patience/

Harris, A. (2022, June 8). *#stayhomestayhopeful - Radical Acceptance in a Time of Uncertainty*. Hopeway.org. https://hopeway.org/blog/radical-acceptance

Institute, N. (2020, September 23). *Social Media Narcissism in Young Adults*. Newport Institute. https://www.newportinstitute.com/resources/mental-health/social-media-narcissism/

International Bipolar Foundation. (n.d.) *50 Ways to Start Practicing Self-Care*. International Bipolar Foundation. Retrieved September 10, 2022, from https://ibpf.org/articles/50-ways-to-start-practicing-self-care/

Jack, C. (2020, June 3). *5 Reasons You're Attracted to Narcissists* Psychology Today. Www.psychologytoday.com. https://www.psychologytoday.com/intl/blog/women-autism-spectrum-disorder/202006/5-reasons-youre-attracted-narcissists

Jennifer. (2019, February 12). *10 Powerful Benefits of Being Patient*. Contentment Questing.

https://contentmentquesting.com/10-powerful-benefits-of-being-patient/

Johnson, L. (2021, August 23). *12 Techniques to Help You Start Your Journey to Self-Discovery.* Oprah Daily. https://www.oprahdaily.com/life/a37374739/journey-to-self-discovery/

Klein P. (2022, January 22). *2 Different Types of Patience.* TwosApp. https://medium.com/twosapp/2-different-types-of-patience-2cd39201ef2b

Lancer, D. (2016, April 24). *What is Narcissistic Abuse?* Psych Central. https://psychcentral.com/lib/what-is-narcissistic-abuse#1

Lawler, M. (2021, May 19). *What is self-care and why is it critical for your health?* EverydayHealth.com. https://www.everydayhealth.com/self-care/

Ledgard, D. (2016, September 3). *3 Reasons Why It is Hard to Move on from an Abusive relationship.* Trauma Counselling. https://trauma-vancouver.com/2016/09/03/abusive-relationship/

Love Is Respect. (n.d.). *Types of abuse. Love Is Respect.* Retrieved September 9, 2022, from https://www.loveisrespect.org/resources/types-of-abuse/

Lowrance, M. (2021, March 8). *6 Types of Boundaries & Questions to Explore Them.* Urban Wellness.

https://urbanwellnesscounseling.com/6-types-of-boundaries/

Mandal, A. (2010, July 12). *Heritability of Narcissism.* News-Medical.net. https://www.news-medical.net/health/Heritability-of-Narcissism.aspx

Mayo Clinic. (n.d.). *Narcissistic personality disorder - Symptoms and causes.* Mayo Clinic. Retrieved September 1, 2022, from https://www.mayoclinic.org/diseases-conditions/narcissistic-personality-disorder/symptoms-causes/syc-20366662#:~:text=Although%20the%20cause%20of%20narcissistic

McDowall, S. (2020, February 19). *Narcissism and the Trauma of Narcissistic Abuse.* Farah Therapy Centre. https://www.farahtherapycentre.co.uk/blog/narcissism-and-the-trauma-of-narcissistic-abuse

Mind Tools Content Team. (n.d.). *Patience: Don't Let Frustration Get the Better of You.* Www.mindtools.com. Retrieved September 10, 2022, from https://www.mindtools.com/pages/article/newTCS_78.htm#:~:text=According%20to%20research%20by%20psychologist

National Domestic Violence Hotline. (n.d.). *The Importance of Self-Care.* The Hotline. Retrieved September 10, 2022, from https://www.thehotline.org/resources/the-importance-of-self-care/

Neff, K. (2015, September 30). *The five myths of self-compassion.* Greater Good. https://greatergood.berkeley.edu/article/item/the_five_myths_of_self_compassion

Neff, K. (2019). *Definition and Three Elements of Self Compassion.* Self-Compassion. https://self-compassion.org/the-three-elements-of-self-compassion-2/

Neuharth, D. (2017, September 8). *12 Classic Propaganda Techniques Narcissists Use to Manipulate You.* Psych Central. https://psychcentral.com/blog/narcissism-decoded/2017/09/12-classic-propaganda-techniques-narcissists-use-to-manipulate-you#1

Onelove. (2017, December 21). *11 Reasons Why People in Abusive Relationships Can't "Just Leave."* One Love Foundation. https://www.joinonelove.org/learn/why_leaving_abuse_is_hard/

Optimum Performance Institute. (n.d.). *Failure to Launch Treatment Program for Young Adults (Ages 17 - 28).* Www.optimumperformanceinstitute.com. Retrieved September 2, 2022, from https://www.optimumperformanceinstitute.com/failure-to-launch-syndrome/#:~:text=Failure%20to%20launch%20syndrome%20is

Osunsanya, S. O. (2016, October 23). *The power of self discovery*. The Guardian Nigeria News - Nigeria and World News. https://guardian.ng/sunday-magazine/the-power-of-self-discovery/

Paglia, D. M. (2020, February 21). *10 Signs You Are in Love with a Narcissist*. IPC. https://theinternationalpsychologyclinic.com/10-signs-you-are-in-love-with-a-narcissist/#:~:text=If%20you%20are%20in%20love

Patience Is a Virtue (2020, June 27). Www.theguesthouseocala.com. https://www.theguesthouseocala.com/patience-is-a-virtue/

Pedersen, T. (2021, March 29). *What Causes Narcissistic Personality Disorder?* Psych Central. https://psychcentral.com/disorders/what-causes-narcissistic-personality-disorder#environment

Ph.D, N. C. (2021, November 13). *How to Begin Your Self-Discovery Journey: 16 Best Questions*. PositivePsychology.com. https://positivepsychology.com/self-discovery/#questions

Polish, J. (2020, August 14). *8 Types Of Self-Care & How To Practice Them, According To Experts*. Bustle. https://www.bustle.com/wellness/types-of-self-care-how-to-practice-experts

Polonia, M. (2019). *3 Elements of Self-Compassion.* Dr. Madeline Polonia. https://www.madelinepolonia.com/blog/3-elements-of-self-compassion

Radhakrishnan, R., & Shaikh, J. (2022, March 2). *What Are 12 Signs of a Narcissist?* MedicineNet; MedicineNet. https://www.medicinenet.com/what_are_12_signs_of_a_narcissist/article.htm

Ratson, M. (2022, May 20). *5 Ways to Leave an Abusive Relationship.* WikiHow. https://www.wikihow.com/Leave-an-Abusive-Relationship

Raypole, C. (2020, July 27). *12 Signs You Might Have Narcissistic Victim Syndrome.* Healthline. https://www.healthline.com/health/narcissistic-victim-syndrome

Riyah Speaks. (2021, March 17). *25 Self Love Affirmations For Building Self Compassion* Riyah Speaks. https://riyahspeaks.com/25-self-love-affirmations-for-self-compassion

Rodgers, L. (2021, January 25). *How to Leave an Abusive Relationship: 18 Expert Tips.* The Healthy. https://www.thehealthy.com/family/relationships/how-to-leave-an-abusive-relationship/

Roy, J. (n.d.). *Boundaries: Definition, Examples & How To Set Them.* The Berkeley Well-Being Institute. Retrieved September 9, 2022, from

https://www.berkeleywellbeing.com/boundarie
s.html

safehorizon. (2017). *Domestic Violence Statistics & Facts.*
Safe   Horizon.
https://www.safehorizon.org/get-
informed/domestic-violence-statistics-
facts/#statistics-and-facts/

Scott, E. (2020, August 3). *5 self-care practices for every area
of your life.* Verywell Mind; Verywell Mind.
https://www.verywellmind.com/self-care-
strategies-overall-stress-reduction-3144729

7 Summit Pathways. (2020, February 27). *What

Is Self-Compassion.* 7 Summit Pathways.

https://7summitpathways.com/blog/what-is-

self-compassion/

Stines, S. (2020, January 13). *Traits Narcissists Appreciate
in   their   Targets.*   Psych   Central.
https://psychcentral.com/pro/recovery-
expert/2020/01/traits-narcissists-appreciate-in-
their-targets#1

Team, G. (2022, June 3). *How to be More Patient: 25 Tips
for Increasing Patience in All Parts of Life.* Goodwall
Blog.   https://www.goodwall.io/blog/how-to-
be-more-
patient/#:~:text=Understand%20What%20Pati
ence%20Is%20and%20Isn

Telloian, C. (2021, September 15). *How Many Types of Narcissism Are There?* Psych Central. https://psychcentral.com/health/types-of-narcissism

The Center for Relationship Abuse Awareness. (2014). *The Center for Relationship Abuse Awareness & Action.* Center for Relationship Abuse Awareness & Action. http://stoprelationshipabuse.org/educated/what-is-relationship-abuse/

The Recovery Village. (2022, May 26). *Signs of Narcissistic Personality Disorder (NPD) Statistics* Learn More. The Recovery Village Drug and Alcohol Rehab. https://www.therecoveryvillage.com/mental-health/narcissistic-personality-disorder/npd-statistics/#:~:text=Narcissism%20Prevalence&text=Most%20teenagers%20display%20narcissistic%20qualities

Tull, M. (2021, May 28). *Living With PTSD? Be Nicer to Yourself.* Verywell Mind. https://www.verywellmind.com/increasing-self-compassion-in-ptsd-2797565

Turino, S. (n.d.). *10 Benefits of Self Care That Might Surprise You.* Sarah Turino. Retrieved September 10, 2022, from https://www.sarahturino.com/blog/10-benefits-of-self-care-that-might-surprise-you

University of North Carolina. (n.d.). *What Self-Compassion is NOT.* Retrieved September 9, 2022, from https://selfcompassion.web.unc.edu/what-is-self-compassion/what-self-compassion-is-not/

University of St. Augustine for health sciences. (2020, April 7). *55+ Self-Discovery Questions for Personal Growth [+ Printables]*. University of St. Augustine for Health Sciences. https://www.usa.edu/blog/self-discovery-questions/

van der Kolk, B. (2014). *The Body Keeps the Score: Mind, Brain and Body in the Transformation of Trauma*. Penguin Books.

wikiHow. (2009, April 4). *Recognize a Potentially Abusive Relationship*. wikiHow. https://www.wikihow.com/Recognize-a-Potentially-Abusive-Relationship

Willowstone family center. (n.d.). *8 Types of Self-Care*. Willowstone Family Services. https://www.willowstone.org/news/8-types-of-self-care

Winters, J. (2016, August 15). *13 Warning Signs You're Falling In Love With A Narcissist*. Thought Catalog. https://thoughtcatalog.com/jessica-winters/2016/08/13-warning-signs-youre-falling-in-love-with-a-narcissist/

Wood, K. (2021, November 15). *7 Traits Narcissists Look for in Their Victims*. Kamini Wood. https://www.kaminiwood.com/7-traits-narcissists-look-for-in-their-victims/

Woods, A. (2020, April 13). *What Are the 3 Essential Elements of Self-Compassion?* Wildhearted. https://www.ashliewoods.com/blog/2020/4/12/what-are-the-3-essential-elements-of-self-compassion

Printed in Great Britain
by Amazon

38405627R00106